# MY LIFE

## Dodging Curve Balls
## Jumping Hurdles
## Getting Surprised

## Lorie Eber

ISBN: 9798333932235

PUBLISHED BY
Lorie Eber Wellness Coaching

# Dedication

I want to thank my trusted support team for helping me get this book to print. Without Judy Rose, my editor/proofer, and Victoria Vinton, my formatter, this book would not have come to life.

I also want to thank my husband Wes for being there for me every day as my best friend and biggest supporter. We are both dealing with new and different challenges as we age, but we are working through them together and that makes all the difference.

# Contents

# Introduction

I've lived most of my life by now. At age 68, I hope I have accumulated some wisdom or at least some relatable experiences to share with you. I admit to being introspective to the point of over analyzing everything ad nauseum. But perhaps that trait has given me the ability to avoid getting stuck in a rut, like a needle in a groove on an old turntable, as I've tried to deal with life's ups and downs.

This book is not an autobiography, but it details the broad outlines of my life experiences, as well as the insights I have drawn from them. Expect the text to jump around a bit and explore a variety of different topics that have significance for me.

## It's Been a Far More Interesting Journey Than I Expected

We never know what to expect in life, but I'm grateful to have my younger years, when I had no idea who I was, what I wanted to do with my time on this planet, or how to get there, in the rear view mirror. At my current age, I've amassed an overstuffed bag of life situations, and feel capable of dodging any curve ball, clearing every hurdle, and dealing with the inevitable surprises. And it's a good thing I have those skills because aging is rife with new and different challenges every day.

In retrospect I didn't have the easiest childhood. I had a mother who went MIA on her children. She even moved away for a year. I envied other kids who had doting parents and imposed rules. That made for a tough start, but I chose to forgive my mother rather than wallow in my sorrow with 30 years of therapy.

At a young age I decided on my career path in law. My choice was spurred by a very unrealistic portrayal of the profession on a television show, but I got lucky and enjoyed my 23 years as a corporate litigator despite the flimsy reasoning.

I did less well in my personal life, getting into a marriage for all the wrong reasons. After seven years, at least I had the good sense to end it when an opportune situation arose. I learned a lot from my marital failure and chose better the second time around.

But here comes to part I am most proud of: I retired from law early and bravely subjected myself to the torture of trying to identify another equally satisfying, purposeful career. At first it was scary, then it was overwhelming, and eventually it turned into a 10-year unexpectedly wonderful adventure.

I've also written about a few other issues. One is enduring pain, since it feels like I've been singled out for more than my fair share. I also have a real issue with that phantom work life balance idea. Most days I feel like I'm running as fast as I can. Try as I might, it seems like I go from overly busy to bored in a split second, without much in the middle. And I place no credence in the idea that making a list of New Year's Resolutions will ever trigger any change in my go-go-go approach.

With that brief synopsis, I wish you happy reading.

# | 1 |

## A Less Than Stellar Childhood

What was your childhood like? While mine was less than stellar, and certainly not the upbringing I'd endeavor to provide for my children had I been brave enough to have any, it could have been a lot worse. There definitely were some happy times as well. Overall, I'd grade it as a C- at best.

### Home Environment

My childhood home was polluted by the sound of my parents' non-stop arguing. Two perennial bones of contention between my parents were that Mom liked to take a nap after work and prepare dinner at her leisure, while my Dad came home starving. Many nights he ended up eating two dinners. The other trigger was that my Dad would be all spiffed up and ready to go out an hour before departure time, while my mother was still on our terrace in her bathing suit soaking up the sun when it was time to leave.

I just wanted them to stop bickering because their acrimony affected me on a visceral level. On my own initiative I felt driven to intervene in these squabbles to preserve my sanity. Perhaps this was my destiny having come out of the womb as one of those weirdly precocious kids who is always serious and studious. Smiling was not in my repertoire in those days.

Early on I assumed a role akin to mediator between Mommy and Daddy. Unfortunately, my attempts at peacemaking were not met with approval by either parent. They ignored my entreaties and continued to fire barbs back and forth, occasionally accenting their venting with a hurled object.

Yet I persisted in my desire for peace and quiet because I needed solace after dealing with the nasty nuns all day at school. Was it too much to ask to be able to focus on my homework without having to block out The Bickersons? Apparently that was a pipe dream that would have meant living in someone else's house. By the time high school rolled around, I'd had enough, and spent almost every evening at a girlfriend's house to avoid going home.

## My Siblings

I have four siblings. One was my buddy—my younger brother, one was my sworn enemy—my older sister, and the other two (a much older half-brother who was in college and a younger sister who was born severely retarded and sent to an institution) did not affect my life very much.

We lived in the typical postage-sized New York City apartment, so my younger brother's room was a cordoned off space designed to be a dining nook. I shared a room with my evil sister and my older brother slept on the couch when he was home from college.

I have treasured memories of spending many hours with my younger brother inspecting, arranging, and meticulously cataloging his baseball cards in shoe boxes. We remained good buds until he went away to college. After sophomore year he got married so he could share a room with his love while they studied abroad. That turned out to be the death knell for our connection since his future wife did not permit female competition for his affection. Sadly, we only speak once a year now and that's because I insist on calling him on his birthday. I think of it as a gift but he probably takes it as a dreaded chore.

My older sister was unremittingly nasty to me. She is only one year older than I so we had a few mutual friends who she did her best to convince that they should unfriend me for life. She took pleasure in beating me up just for fun. Even though she is small in stature, she was an accurate and relentless kicking machine and delivered such painful blows that I appealed to Dad for help. He brushed me off, saying "Learn to fight your own battles."

In fairness, perhaps I have an evil streak in me just like my sister. After all, I did kill one of her pet mice out of spite. Here's what happened. She was constantly bringing home small pets like hamsters and guinea pigs and even a snake. She also bred a mouse colony in our bedroom. The critters were so prolific that every flat surface in our shared room was covered with cages of the varmints running noisily on hamster wheels as if they had an important place to be.

As a night-owl, my sister favored doing her chores after midnight when I was fast asleep. That's when she decided to tackle the task of cleaning and fumigating the rodents' cages. In the meantime, the mice were set free to run around our bedroom, which sent a few of them scurrying for cover in the warmth of my bed. Being abruptly awakened from a deep sleep by the sensation of a mouse crawling on me became a dreaded part of my teenage years.

One day in a fit of exasperation, opportunity knocked. I was closing the closet's folding doors and a mouse just happened to be in the wrong place at precisely the wrong time. I'll admit that I didn't shed any tears over my population control efforts, but my sister was none too pleased. While I'm not terribly proud of committing rodenticide, my bad deed did not cause me any sleepless nights.

As adults my sister and I have put the past behind us but I wouldn't say that we are bffs. We have a pleasant superficial relationship. She has even given me (belated) credit for teaching her a semester's worth of Latin in one evening, enabling her to pass the course.

My much older half-brother didn't take kindly to being tasked with babysitting us littler rug rats. When he had to take us somewhere I had to practically break into a run or he'd leave me in his dust, which was what he fervently hoped for. We probably looked like three toy poodles pumping their legs into a blur of activity.

My younger sister was born severely mentally retarded (that was the nomenclature at the time and I still use it). I remember her crawling around on the floor but never walking, talking, or eating on her own. No one ever talked about her condition. I later was told that her brain was deprived of oxygen during the delivery process. My parents never filed a malpractice lawsuit. It just wasn't done in those days.

At some point she was placed in a care facility. She is now in her 60s and lives in a group home in Albany, N.Y. run by Catholic Charities. I went through a laborious court process to be designated as her guardian because no one else wanted to take responsibility for making sure that her needs were being met.

## My Mom

My Mom was emotionally unavailable, to put it kindly. She was unwilling or incapable of accepting parental responsibility. Instead, she treated us as younger siblings whose role was to keep her company while she enjoyed the finer things in life. I was dragged to all the finest museums, symphonies, and ballets New York City had to offer. She wanted to travel abroad, so she took each of us on a European vacation. But providing day-to-day care for her children was not of any particular interest to her.

Here are a few lowlights that emphasize the level of her neglect. I recall one time when she allowed my hair to get so tangled that she had to cut out the snarls, leaving me with a very odd-looking hairdo.

Explaining the birds and bees was never on Mom's to-do list. The first time I got my period I was petrified. Luckily my evil sister took pity on me and calmed me down.

I knew better than to ask my mother's permission to do anything since she didn't seem to care what I did. The only advice she ever gave me was not to get fat and not to get married. She was not the type of mom I could confide in to help me deal with the typical teenage issues.

When I was in the fourth grade, we were living in DC because of Dad's job. Mom suddenly disappeared. Naturally we were given no explanation for her absence. Years later, when I was an adult, my Dad dropped a bombshell and revealed that she had gone to live with her lover in New York City, which was in line with her philandering ways. Out of a sense of misguided responsibility, Dad put up with Mom's bad behavior. About a year later, he was able to get a job transfer and moved us to the Big Apple, where she rejoined us without discussion. The sad thing is that her absence hardly affected me at all and I just assumed it was normal to go bra shopping with my Dad.

When I was in my 50s, my Dad laid another stunner on me. He disclosed that Mom once left me alone in a playpen in the backyard. When it started raining, the neighbors heard my wailing and called Child Protective Services. By Dad's telling, he was annoyed with me, not with my mother, because the incident necessitated hiring an attorney to maintain custody. Luckily I have no recollection of that potentially traumatic event.

I longed for the kind of relationship that my friends had with their mothers but that was not to be. Since kids are narcissists, I naturally assumed that there

4

was something wrong with me that caused her to dislike me. I remember sobbing to my high school yoga teacher about what a terrible person I must be since even my mother hated me. She knew just what to say in the moment and helped me get over my feelings of rejection and abandonment. I was able to make peace with the fact that my MIA Mom was not an evil person, but just a totally inept parent.

## My Dad

Thank the Lord that my Dad was a twofer: a dad and a mom in a single package. He was the family breadwinner and also a darn good stand-in mother. I later learned that his nurturing skills were developed at a young age when he volunteered to babysit for his two young nephews.

Dad worked for the Feds so he was reliably home at 5:30 every evening. As a small child, I remember staring out the window eagerly anticipating the sight of his car pulling up and breaking into a run to hop up on top of his immaculate dress shoes so he could pick me up as soon as he crossed the threshold.

One of my favorite memories is of a time when I was at home sick and Dad had gone to the car dealership to buy a new car. When he came back Mom lifted me up to see a brand new Rambler in my favorite shade of pink. I'm sure that loving gesture sped up my recovery.

When I was a teenager Dad bought a foldable ping pong table that took up the entire expanse of our living room. He was only five-feet tall and never athletic, but he had excellent hand-eye coordination and the family spent many evenings batting that little plastic ball from side to side.

My other rosy childhood memory was a stroke of genius. Dad had tired of trying to guess which Christmas toys each of us wanted and came up with an inspired means of ending the squabbling about who got the better gifts from Santa. His solution was to lay out the humungous Sears catalog and give each of us a budget with instructions to select whatever toys suited our fancy. It headed off a lot of tantrums as we grabbed our presents from under the tree and served as an introduction to financial basics at an early age.

# Looking Back

Clearly I did not have the idyllic *Leave it to Beaver*, *Father Knows Best* upbringing. I lacked any real mothering and was forced to mature at an early age since my parents failed to set any rules for me. I wanted to be one of those kids who had a curfew or was prohibited from going to that high school dance where I ended up in an unsafe sexual situation and had to beg the cops not to drive me home. I yearned to feel guided and protected.

I did my best to navigate life at a tender age and am thankful I was blessed with fairly decent common sense. I rode the subways at all hours but was savvy enough to be on the alert for dangerous looking characters and to steer clear of trouble. One terrible encounter with hard liquor in the park taught me to respect alcohol. I didn't always do too well choosing boyfriends, but was able to avoid any serious life-changing trouble like an unwanted pregnancy.

All and all, I did fairly well making my own decisions, falling on my face periodically and getting back up. I came into adulthood feeling fully capable of handling anything that came my way with confidence.

# | 2 |

## Two Quite Different Careers So Far: Law

When people learn about my background, they are surprised and curious about my career path. After all, it's quite an outside-the-box move to go from being a corporate litigator to opening up a wellness coaching practice. But then I've never been terribly concerned about complying with societal norms.

I want to give you a flavor for my legal career so that you don't leap to the conclusion that I never liked being a lawyer and that's why I cast aside the legal mantle and veered off in an entirely different direction.

### My Legal Career Was Spurred by a Television Show

One evening when I was watching television, I happened upon the courtroom crime drama *Perry Mason*. From the first viewing, I definitely knew the answer to the question "What do you want to be when you grow up?" I was thoroughly captivated by the TV version of legal practice depicted in the program. Every week Raymond Burr shocked a deceitful witness with cold hard facts that his detective had fortuitously discovered just moments earlier, leading to a dramatic breakdown and confession on the stand. Practicing law looked like so much fun that it was very easy to cast aside my childhood female inclination to become a teacher. Why not be a hotshot lawyer?

After enduring two years each at Penn State and San Francisco State with the most amorphous major ever—Interdisciplinary Studies in Social Sciences, I enrolled in Hastings College of the Law in San Francisco mainly because the price and location were right.

I hated law school right from the beginning because it was more about memorization than thinking and analyzing and the classes were huge. But I did surprisingly well, despite overindulging in pot to give myself a mental break from the tedious studying. By the time I was taking the bar review course, I'd adopted running as a healthier coping mechanism.

## My Chicago Detour

My plan after passing the bar was to move to Chicago to live with my old law school boyfriend and give it a trial run. But I hedged my bets and took the California bar, keeping my options open in case love did not prevail.

As I began my legal career, I realized that law school had left me woefully unprepared to practice law, so the fact that my firm offered a robust training program for new associates was a welcome relief. But I also wanted the opportunity to put that knowledge to work. I've never been good at "hurry up and wait." Fear and intimidation fester in me the longer I'm relegated to watching and not doing. I yearned to be in the hot seat, taking depositions, negotiating settlements, and trying cases. I wanted to live my *Perry Mason* fantasy.

Unfortunately, getting real-world experience didn't happen on "Lorie time" because the firm specialized in extremely complex administrative matters involving mega millions. Therefore, green peas like me were assigned relatively low-level grunt work which I felt any competent paralegal could have handled.

Finally, in year three, I got the opening I'd been looking for. The firm had been retained to represent one of the major defendants in the multi-district litigation arising out of the MGM Grand fire which had swept through the hotel like a tornado when the inadequate sprinkler system had failed. Since 85 people had died in the conflagration, dozens of depositions were scheduled every day, so it was all hands on deck.

Before I knew it, I'd been relocated to Las Vegas sharing a condo with two other attorneys. I was thrilled to have the opportunity to finally acquire real lawyering skills. My first depositions proved a bit challenging because I found myself competing with loudly thumping heavy metal music emanating from the aerobics studio below our rented space. But I was pleased that I was finally growing and developing in my chosen profession.

I managed to stick it out for three long brutal winters and sweltering summers in Chicago. But by that time, I'd come to realize that neither my law firm position nor my live-in beau was a good fit. It was time to return to California.

## My Return to California

I did a blitzkrieg of interviews in San Francisco in just a few days, got an attractive offer from a mid-sized firm, accepted it immediately, and moved back to the Bay Area. Within the first few weeks on the job I realized that I'd been assigned to work for the nastiest partner in the firm, a man who had a richly deserved reputation for burning through associates.

While his periodic outbursts and unwarranted criticisms were upsetting, I stayed with the firm because working with this caustic senior partner had a major upside: career development. On my first day of work, he motioned toward a bank of about two dozen case files and told me those were mine. While this should have frightened me to death given the fact that I'd never had sole responsibility for a single case before, I embraced the opportunity and took solace in the fact that a few rookie errors probably wouldn't produce any dire consequences because they were relatively small dollar cases. I faked it 'til I made it, all the while gaining the necessary confidence to handle the more complex matters I would work on a few years later.

## Lawyering is Fun

Once I was afforded the opportunity to run my own cases and handle client contact, I began to feel that I was in my element and that I'd chosen the profession that was perfect for me. The reality of practice was not *Perry Mason*-like but I loved working with other smart lawyers and solving clients' problems. I never became cocky or arrogant or flattered myself into thinking I was a genius just because I'd successfully slogged my way through law school and passed the bar exam. Nor did I delude myself into thinking that my legal expertise was a credential that should garner automatic admiration and respect. My take was that being a good attorney required nothing more than learning the ins and outs of how the legal system worked and mastering the profession's vernacular, neither of which requires Mensa intelligence.

I found that I really enjoyed plowing through mounds of documents produced by opposing counsel, spurred by the tantalizing possibility of discovering the "smoking gun" document intentionally buried under a pile of meaningless paper.

I learned how to cajole useful information out of witnesses in depositions and prided myself on my ability to get an unsuspecting deponent to spill the beans without realizing he'd put his foot in his mouth.

Many male attorneys took one look at me and mistakenly presumed they'd be able to push me around. What they didn't know was that this tough New Yorker is not easily intimidated. At the first sign of nasty, aggressive behavior from opposing counsel, I morphed into take-no-prisoners mode. Attorneys who chose to saber-rattle with me generally only tried it once and then wrote me off as an incorrigible bitch not to be toyed with.

This was an enjoyable game to me. I could switch attitudes quickly. Just as soon as the sworn testimony concluded, I reverted to my normal persona and extended my hand in peace much like Federer and Nadal after a hard-fought tennis match.

I worked in a defense firm, a business enterprise that makes money when lawyers bill time to client files. To further encourage profit-making activity, the company established a strict billing minimum that associates were expected to meet or be shown the door.

During the week I often switched on the office lights in the morning and burned the midnight oil after hours. For many years I prided myself on being the highest biller in the firm. I'd made a decision to prioritize my career over my personal life. I was a certified workaholic and perfectly comfortable with my choice.

With no mentor to guide me, I operated under the fallacious assumption that if I worked my tail off, did an exemplary job on my cases, volunteered to take on more work, and billed tons of hours, I'd be invited to join the boys' club. I'd focused all my energies on making partner in a male law firm. Failure was not an option.

## You'll Never Believe How I Made Partner

Like many businesswomen, no one clued me in to the unspoken rules for clawing my way up the corporate ladder. I knew that as a woman trying to reach the top rung, I'd have a more challenging ascent, but I was okay with that. I operated with the blind faith that somehow I'd break the glass. But I kept getting passed over for partnership year after year. Finally I mustered the courage to ask, "What do I need to do to make partner?" The answer threw me for a loop. I was told that my deficit was in my public speaking skills. While I was puzzled by the response, at least now I had something definitive to address.

I wasted no time scouring the Yellow Pages for Speech Pathologists. I selected Dr. Carol Fleming who touted her specialty as communications counseling. When I filled her in on my situation, she seemed intrigued by the unusual challenge.

The partners insisted on interviewing Dr. Fleming over lunch to see if she met their high standards. What they didn't know was that she was psychoanalyzing them. She concluded that their real reservation about letting me into the male fraternity was that they considered my physical appearance unprofessional. I trusted the doctor's intuition.

She outlined a battle plan worthy of a response to the Japanese attack on Pearl Harbor. First a wardrobe consultant did a blitzkrieg through my closet and ordered me to donate 90% of my outfits to Goodwill. Then we went on a shopping spree at a very expensive professional women's boutique and bought some beautifully tailored imported suits and blouses. My transformation was completed with a fashionably short stylish haircut that seemed to reshape my face, a professional make-up session, and earring holes poked through my lobes.

My new 'do, expensive wardrobe, girly face, and new bling didn't elicit any explicit affirmation, but the partners had definitely taken notice and were treating me differently. I was more often greeted with smiles and felt eyes following me as I walked away.

Lo and behold, at my next yearly review, the door swung open and I was welcomed to the inner sanctum. I only wish I'd been savvy enough to figure out the stumbling block earlier. I could have saved myself several years of self-doubt and angst.

Next up: I continue my journey with an unusual twist.

# | 3 |

## Two Quite Different Careers: Wellness Coaching

Even after finally making partner, I continued my workaholic ways, totally devoting myself to my career and even volunteering to set up and run a new office in SoCal. I'm still astounded that I figured out how to build a successful branch office.

### Why I Decided to Give Up the Big Bucks

I started to notice that after 23 years, I felt like I had nothing left to prove and had to admit that I was no longer champing at the bit to get to the office and slave away.

Once I've conquered a challenge, I get bored. I hate being bored and I like to go out on top. The last thing I wanted was to hang on and turn into one of those lawyers the profession derisively refers to as "dead wood," who contribute very little to the firm but continue to occupy that coveted corner office. I didn't feel ready to pull the plug yet but I needed to find a way to be excited about my job once again.

While I was wrestling with these feelings, karma intervened. I met my soulmate at the gym. We got married in record time and unlike marriage #1 (which I'll be discussing later on), this was one was worth nurturing.

When I came home after being the Boss Lady of the office all day, I tried my darnedest to de-stress and act like a normal person. Yet clearly my transformation was underwhelming because almost every evening my new husband calmly reminded me that he was not my secretary. Try as I might, I was unable to leave my in-charge attitude in the office and assume my loving wife role when I crossed the threshold.

I began wondering if continuing to practice law and creating a good marriage were mutually exclusive goals. Perhaps I was simply incapable of tamping down the stress of legal practice to a level that allowed me to appropriately prioritize my personal life. Since I am saddled with a Type A personality, the only way I know how to work is to do things full-bore; to leave no stone unturned. After all, that's how a perfectionist behaves.

The more I ruminated about where I was in life, the more that "been there, done that" syndrome began to take hold in my psyche. As I battled with the pros and cons of walking away from such a lucrative career, I realized that the bigger issue was that doing so violated my long-held feminist tenet of jealously guarding my financial independence.

I'd never even envisioned depending on a man to support me. And my recent nasty divorce wasn't very far off in my rear-view mirror. But I also realized that my new marriage was different. I expected it to last forever and had total confidence in my husband's ability to support me. I reasoned that if I gave up the big bucks and changed careers, I'd be self-supporting again in a short time. Admittedly, I would probably never achieve the same level of income, but I assumed that finding another purposeful job would happen fairly expeditiously.

I agonized about this decision for some months and beat the subject to death with my new husband who was pushing me to put my legal career behind me and decrease my stress. I finally bit the bullet and announced my "retirement" at the age of 49. My partners' reactions ranged from shock to jealousy. Several of them, including many who were quite a bit younger than I, confided that they would follow me out the door in a heartbeat if they weren't constrained by their financial obligations. Many were the sole support for their wives and children, so they didn't have the option of getting out any time soon.

Quite a few of my partners asked me to stay on part-time, and others assumed I'd just gone wacko and would come to my senses. To a man, they expressed disbelief that the biggest workaholic in the firm would resign from the practice 16 years before normal retirement age. A rumor began floating around that someone had started a betting pool on the date I'd realize I'd made a precipitous decision and return to the fold. But I did not waiver in my decision and have never regretted it.

Legal practice had been the perfect occupation for me and satisfied my need to demonstrate to myself that I had the chops to be a big-time attorney. The actual day-to-day practice felt more like skilled gamesmanship than an endeavor that called for esoteric knowledge. Lawyering also involves a lot of grunt work, but I took that in stride and eventually learned how to delegate most of it. I had a good run with my first career, but it was time to identify a new venture that would get my juices flowing again and re-inject a fulfilling sense of purpose into my life. Hopefully it would come with at least a modest paycheck.

## My Journey in Search of a New Me

I knew I was now in uncharted territory since the only version of me had been "Lorie the Lawyer." When I gave up that sense of myself, I felt empty and directionless as if I were bobbing around in the ocean clueless as to how to get back to shore. After quelling the worst of the panic, I began facing the formidable task of sorting through the overwhelming number of choices in my effort to identify a new rewarding career that would allow for a personal life on the side. With learning to play golf as my only distraction, I reached back to one of my comfort zones—education.

No way was I revisiting campus life a second time. I enrolled in a fully online program in Aging Studies offered by a local community college. I was aware that the population was aging rapidly and reasoned that the demographics would open up a wide variety of career opportunities. I was optimistic that there must be some position in the field that would match my skills and interests.

I was also driven by a personal experience. I had just moved my Dad, who was exhibiting preliminary signs of dementia, into an assisted living facility and was surprised at how difficult it was to navigate the tangled web of elder care services

In addition to my studies, I wanted exposure to potential career options so I could try them on for size. I decided to volunteer at the Council on Aging in the Ombudsman Program despite the daunting 35-hour mandatory training program. This unpaid position required visiting assisted living and skilled nursing homes, acting as an advocate for the residents, investigating claims of abuse, and reporting serious issues to the regulatory authorities. I liked the mission and found it a good fit for my legal background.

Being an ombudsman turned out to be a very difficult and sometimes acrimonious uncompensated assignment. But I carried out my assigned duties diligently and the Program Manager took note and brought me on as a part-time paid staffer. In a short period of time I was offered the position of Ombudsman Trainer and Recruiter. In typical Lorie fashion, I revamped the entire program, thus creating a lot of extra work for myself. But the end result was more than worth the time investment. I enjoyed using my long dormant creative skills to invent engaging skits and role plays and to fashion them into a more participatory hands-on program. While in this position, I discovered that I had a knack for, and greatly enjoyed, developing curriculum and teaching.

After a six-year stint at the Council, I became disenchanted with the way the well-meaning but under qualified staff ran the organization. I wanted to get out of the non-profit world and back into the business environment where I was more comfortable.

Meanwhile, as I was finishing up my online program at the college, I was unexpectedly given entrée into teaching. The Department Chair was looking for someone to create and teach a non-credit class for older adults. Although the compensation was minimal, I saw this opportunity as a gift, accepted the challenge, and then tried to figure out how to do what I'd signed up for.

Creating the course from scratch turned out to be the easy part. What I hadn't realized was that I was also responsible for attracting the students. Even though this was a free course, getting students in the chairs turned out to be far more difficult than I'd imagined. But it was satisfying work and I hoped it might lead to a permanent teaching position in the Aging Studies Department.

Lo and behold, after a few semesters of teaching in the Adult Education Department, I was invited to teach the Introduction to Aging Studies class in the general curriculum. That led to a regular online teaching assignment that has yielded a steady supplemental income since 2006.

## My Transition Took 10 Years

As I slowly discovered my burgeoning skills and abilities, I tried out a myriad of potential career options, including writing about elder care issues online and for local papers. I was also hired by a healthy aging website to expound on the benefits of eating particular foods to enhance health.

I tried my hand at paid and unpaid public speaking opportunities, found that this was something I was good at and enjoyed, but ultimately realized that I disliked the traveling and marketing efforts required to secure them.

Finally it occurred to me that health and wellness had been an area of intense interest to me for as long as I could remember. So naturally I proceeded to over educate myself in that field, obtaining a surfeit of certifications in personal training, nutrition, life coaching, and wellness coaching.

As soon as I began studying the field of wellness coaching, which is based on helping people with their health using behavior change techniques, I knew that the search was over and that my eureka moment had happened. This would be my new career. It felt much like the career version of finding a soulmate. After completing two wellness coaching programs, I bravely set up my business, named it "Lorie Eber Wellness Coaching," and by trial and error slowly learned how to run a business and attract clients. I've beaten the odds for start-ups, having just logged my 11th year in my mission-driven career.

To add icing to the cake, a few years ago a new Dean was hired by the college who happens to have a passion for health and wellness. I cajoled him into permitting me to develop and teach two health and wellness courses. So now my teaching is in sync with my health-driven mission as well.

## In Retrospect

My post-law decade-long journey has been far more gratifying than I'd ever dreamed possible. I feel extraordinarily lucky to have the luxury to live out my passion every day, and feel a rewarding sense of purpose.

I have a much more balanced life these days. My greatest happiness will always come from my marriage. I'm still dumbfounded that I found my true love, always having assumed that I'd have to settle for someone who did not truly understand me. Life doesn't get any better than this!

# | 4 |

# I Was a Latecomer to Giving Health Its Due

For a considerable part of my life, I didn't pay much attention to my health. Why bother when I felt fine and was able to keep my weight under relatively decent control? I was far more concerned with things like making partner and jamming all my personal chores into my only day off.

My experience is typical. We just assume our health will take care of itself in the same way that the Energizer Bunny's batteries will never run out of juice. Our bodies encourage this delusion by tolerating a great deal of abuse before showing the effects of our bad behavior. But if we ignore our God-given temple too long, there will be a breaking point and we will get our comeuppance.

Please allow me to share my personal health journey with you to demonstrate that you can improve your health even if you were snoozing when the starter's pistol went off.

## I Was a Latecomer to Exercise

Growing up in the DC suburbs, I did the usual kid stuff like riding my bike and cruising the neighborhood on metal roller skates. In school I played at recess but that was it for movement. The nuns weren't much interested in promoting organized sports for girls.

When we left DC and moved to New York City, my couch potato ways continued. The all-girls Catholic high school I attended was housed in twin brownstones and had no outdoor space for exercise. The Sisters' idea of a PE offering was a Friday yoga class in the auditorium which was more about stretching and meditating and less about elevated heart rates. The activities I participated in were all sedentary: chess club, the school newspaper, and choir. After school I went home, planted myself at my desk, and did all my homework. It never occurred to my parents that some physical activity might be good for me. Instead, I was told that my sole job was to study hard, get straight A's, and become a doctor or a lawyer.

The only deviation was during the summer, when my parents wanted a break and shipped us off to camp on Cape Cod for two months. While that may sound idyllic, Camp Manomet had been selected based on its cheap price. When the summer started, there was a wide range of activities including water skiing, archery, and horseback riding. But after a few short weeks the arrows were all broken, the water skis were missing, and most of the horses were lame. For the rest of the summer, we were sent to the beach to get sunburned, undoubtedly laying the foundation for skin cancer 20 years down the line.

My college years at Penn State were similarly bereft of physical activity. I took only the mandatory PE class. The thought of voluntarily participating in any sports was not even on my radar screen. Walking to class was the only movement in my repertoire.

On trips back to NYC during my college years, I occupied myself by taking educational classes at the "Y" and meeting up with old friends for lunch or dinner. The only saving grace was that Manhattanites walk a lot because it's often the most expeditious way to get around.

After I dropped out of Penn State and moved to San Francisco with my former druggie boyfriend, I was a bit more active, although sporadically. We tried to play tennis on the city courts when we could get one and tossed around a softball or pretended to shoot hoops from time to time. When the MUNI went on strike for over two months, I walked the 4.3 miles each way to my job on Market Street. But that was just an aberration.

## I Accidentally Discover the Joys of Exercise

I discovered exercise by accident in my second year of law school when I got myself a new boyfriend who was former military and working on a second career as an attorney. He was disciplined about everything and had a body to die for. After a while I spent most nights in his apartment near Golden Gate Park.

Every day at the crack of dawn he'd get up, quietly sneak out of the bedroom and go for a jog in the park. When he returned, he was sweaty and beaming from ear to ear. I became intrigued about what was plastering that big smile on his face, so one fateful day I asked if I could tag along.

Not surprisingly, just trying to jog the short distance to the park entrance left me winded. But I persevered and headed to the Polo Field to try to complete the 0.8-mile loop. I had to stop before I was even half-way around. But I was motivated to keep at it and embraced the challenge. Soon enough my boyfriend had acquired a running buddy.

Running became a staple in my life for the next several decades. I loved the fact that all I had to do was throw on some running clothes, lace up my shoes, and head out. I could keep it up when I was out of town or got stuck at the office late. I developed a routine of hitting the pavement 5 days a week and running 5 miles. Over the years I participated in many 10ks and ran the Bay to Breakers quite a few times just for fun.

Eventually I expanded my fitness horizons by joining a gym where I took aerobics classes and learned how to lift weights. When I lived in the Marina District of San Francisco I bought a bicycle and cruised around the city on Sundays. I even learned how to navigate the somewhat intimidating ride across the Golden Gate Bridge.

During those intervening years I met and married my first husband (more about him later). We lived in the Bay Area and my older brother also lived nearby.

Eventually, I bought a house and moved to Marin County where I became quite the avid cyclist. My husband and I would pedal out Lucas Valley Road for hours on Sundays, stopping at the Bovine Bakery to refuel and head home. My brother got me involved in organized century rides in the wine country and I even participated in his annual 70+ mile ride around Lake Tahoe. Vacations were Backroads Cycling Tours in New Mexico, the California Wine County, and the San Juan Islands.

Since then I have changed up my activities many times, running the gamut from being a gym-rat for 24 years, to becoming a Covid-shutdown-inspired returnee to running, to dabbling in Pilates, and finally to joining a local spin gym. More recently I have made more intentional changes to accommodate my aging body such as ditching my free weights for stretch bands to avoid injury. I still need to add balance activities to my routine but I haven't figured out that one yet.

## I Eat for Flavor and Convenience

I also showed up late to healthy eating. I've been blessed with a fairly fast metabolism but cursed with a wicked sweet tooth. The first time I paid any attention to my eating habits was the summer of my senior year in high school. I was headed off to Penn State in the fall, facing a lot of unknowns including an assigned roommate. I didn't like the way I looked. I was overweight and there was no denying the fact that I'd been bursting out of my Catholic school uniform by the time I'd graduated. I was determined to show up at college looking more presentable.

I had a sneaking suspicion that the cause of my weight gain was too many trips to the Woolworth's lunch counter where I often indulged in a 3-scoop banana split with all the trimmings. I decided to cold-turkey that treat and miraculously, by the time I went off to college, I was presentable again.

I'd made an unusual dietary change as an impressionable teenager after reading *Diary for a Small Planet* and becoming persuaded that shunning meat was a superior lifestyle. While this created quite a challenge for my mother, particularly when I got my younger brother to join me, I didn't really care. Becoming "vegetarian" wasn't a hardship for me because I could continue to indulge in my favorite food groups—carbs, dairy, and desserts, while telling myself I was saving the world.

As you've probably surmised, my dietary choices for most of my life have been based on eating as much tasty food as I could get away with. During my legal career, lunch at the office was a quick grab-n-go. The closest option was a sandwich shop where I'd pick up a Saran wrapped turkey sandwich on white

24

bread with mayo and a piece of carrot cake. When I was really pressed for time, my secretary would heat up a frozen dinner and I'd scarf it down mindlessly while continuing to bill hours.

By the time I got home in the evening, it was practically bedtime and I was famished. My go-to was a heaping bowl of buttered popcorn with grated Parmesan on top.

Weekends were the time to splurge on cheesy veggie pizzas, over-sized bean burritos, indulgent brunches, and lots of donuts, muffins, and ice cream treats. I enjoyed following the hotshot chefs and trying out their new restaurants.

## I Reform My Diet

I finally got tired of eating popcorn for dinner every night and also became a bit concerned that I'd break a tooth on a partially popped kernel, so I decided to teach myself to cook. I gravitated to Indian food because of the flavorful spices. I was surprised to find myself enjoying the creativity and the reward of an immediate edible result—quite a nice contrast to practicing law. I'd cook on Sunday, make enough for an army, and eat leftovers during the week. This was definitely a nutritional upgrade from popcorn.

After 14 years of the "vegetarianism" farce that I'd perpetrated, I realized that avoiding healthy proteins was making my life unnecessarily difficult, especially when dining out where I was limited to eating whatever tasteless limp vegetables they could rustle up. My motivation to save the world was waning and I had to admit that I really didn't care if chickens got decapitated and eaten by humans.

I slowly reintroduced fish and lean meats to my diet. But to this day I still avoid red meat, because it requires way too much chewing and a dinner plate should not be bloodied.

However, in terms of really cleaning up my diet, that was still a ways off. When I married my second husband about 20 years ago and retired from practicing law, domestic life didn't include spending hours in the kitchen. Neither of us wanted to cook. So for the first eight years of our marriage we ate out almost every night. Even though we tried to make healthy choices, living on restaurant-prepared buttery, oily, salty food is not a prescription for a healthy life. In retrospect, I'm amazed that I didn't gain 25 lbs. during that time. Eventually we got burned out on the restaurant scene and found our way to preparing food at home without making it a time consuming cook-from-scratch ordeal. Getting a barbecue grill was the first step, followed by frequenting the prepared foods section at Whole Foods.

Mediterranean or flexitarian is the best description of my current diet, which focuses on God-made over man-made food. I eat a lot of fruits and vegetables as well as whole grains and lean proteins. Predictably, my formerly speedy metabolism has hit the skids. I've adjusted by severely limiting sweets and giving up alcohol entirely. My dinner plate overflows with every variety of vegetable known to man, but I also make sure I eat my protein. I buy every weird new spice that Trader Joe's invents, and if all else fails, I add salsa or Gochujang sauce to perk things up.

## A Long as You're Above Ground There's Still Time

Now that I've disclosed the gory details of my poor eating habits and long-delayed appearance on the exercise bandwagon, I hope I've convinced you that it's never too late to start making your health a priority.

Changing health habits in today's world is a big challenge since we tend to get caught up in the whirlwind of daily life and it's so easy to take advantage of all the convenient, readily available restaurant-prepared food. But remember that health matters more than anything else in life and even throwing your amassed fortune at your sick body won't put Humpty Dumpty back together again.

The good news is that you have the rest of your life to get healthy, one day at a time. The bad news is that getting and staying healthy requires hard work. We all work hard in many other areas of our lives. Maybe it's time to apply those skills to work on the most valuable thing in life.

# | 5 |

## Lorie's Marital Advice #1

I've decided to share my "wisdom" on marital happiness in honor of my 20 year anniversary in a very happy relationship. Perhaps some reader might benefit from my failures. Things are always obvious in hindsight and the stark differences between husband #1 and my current life partner could not be more apparent. I certainly could have saved myself a lot of heartache had I understood more about what matters in this dance we call marriage.

### Choose Wisely

I've stolen this phrase from Dr. Laura, a radio psychologist who gave marital advice to call-in listeners on a syndicated radio show before she got booted for violating the rules of PC-dom. If I'd discovered her sooner I probably would not have married Richard. Looking back, I'm not sure how I managed to tune out all the screeching sirens that were going off before we ended up at City Hall and did the deed. A lot of my tone-deafness derived from my mindset that at the ripe old age of 36, I was over-due to graduate from serial monogamy and past-due to partner up, settle down, and buy a house in the burbs.

Before I made this colossal error, I'd dated Richard for one year. I'd met him at the bus stop and soon talking turned into romance. Our first date was a bike ride over the Golden Gate bridge into Marin, which I thought boded well. Not only did he look like Tom Selleck, he was also geographically desirable and seemed to have a lot of time for me, magically appearing cruising around on his bike whenever I set foot out the door.

## My First Try

We dated for a year and to my surprise, he proposed marriage on our first anniversary. I was taken aback since we'd never broached the topic and I didn't feel ready. Thankfully he was too cheap to present me with a ring which would have carried the expectation of an immediate answer. After I recovered my bearings, I told him that I needed some time to think about it and made a hasty exit.

In my gut I knew I had serious doubts about whether Richard was the person with whom I wanted to wake up every day forever. I chose to ignore the deafening alarm bells and allowed my analytical brain to kick in to solve a dilemma that should have centered around feelings. Today it seems so glaringly obvious that if you need to resort to a spreadsheet to figure out whether this is the man of your dreams, the answer is definitely a big fat N-O.

Instead, I continued with my analytical evaluation of Richard's husbandly attributes. The man did have many positives: he was attractive and kind, a great workout partner, and a very thoughtful, dependable person. Yet when I allowed reality to busrt through, I had to admit that we did not have good communication. He talked in vague, 60s hippie jargon that sounded like "blah, blah, blah" to me. As a result, I didn't have a good handle on his intelligence level but told myself that he couldn't be a total dolt since he was in grad school and worked as an Economist for the Department of Labor.

The elephant in the room was his relationship with his mother. Richard's Dad had recently died and he lived in his Mom's basement apartment. Even more concerning was that she still cooked all his meals and washed his clothes. For his part, he acted as a devoted son, handyman, and companion. But since he was the matrimonial instigator, I wanted to believe that he was emotionally prepared to make the transition from mama's boy to adoring husband.

Still torn, I realized that I had an ace in the hole. His mother might put the kibosh on this marriage once she learned that I had no intention of producing any grandchildren for her to dote on. I fully expected that she'd freak out if her one and only son married a career woman intent on exterminating her proudly ethnic Italian family name. Yet much to my astonishment and dismay, Richard reported that his mother liked me and was fine with us not having any children. My only escape hatch had slammed shut and I was forced to make my own decision after all.

## It Goes South Immediately

Driven more by my selfish desire to "settle down," than my purportedly objective assessment of his husbandly attributes, I crossed my fingers, hoped for the best, and said "yes." Off we went to City Hall for the legalities, followed by a lovely reception at an upscale vegetarian restaurant. I wasted no time establishing my new life. We bought a house in Marin County with my money, moved in, and were headed off on a meticulously planned two-week honeymoon in Italy, which including staying with some of my new husband's extended family in Lucca.

The day before we were scheduled to embark, there was a hiccup. Richard said, "Maybe we should just go to Tahoe for a few days." He offered no explanation. After I picked my jaw up off the floor and expressed my consternation, I played judge and decreed the suggestion "overruled."

We flew off to the Mediterranean and he made my life miserable. How could anyone be despondent gallivanting around Italy? As it turned out, I'd chosen that one in a million person. He pouted through the cloudy and rainy days and laid the weather blame on me. The expression on my face was, as they say in the Mastercard ad, "priceless." Although I constantly offered Richard his plane ticket home, he preferred to stay and torture me. Without fail, he called his Mommy each and every day to check in with her.

Things did not get better once we returned home. Our marriage played second fiddle to Richard's relationship with his Mom. She remained the center of his universe. If a light bulb burned out, he'd hop in his car, drive into the City, and replace it immediately. Every morning as we commuted together to our respective offices, he insisted that I take a detour to his mother's house so he could assure himself that the building was still standing as he ran up the stairs to kiss his mother. Even more upsetting was the fact that unbeknownst to me, I was expected to spend my paltry non-work time attending a non-stop barrage of family gatherings. If I attempted to opt out, he'd go ballistic. Instead of a peaceful refuge, our home became a place I dreaded returning to after a long hard day at the office.

After years of pointless marriage counseling borne from my desire not to be a marital failure, I belatedly accepted the reality that my husband was still tethered to his role of devoted son and protector of his mother.

31

Then karma intervened. I volunteered to open the SoCal branch office of my law firm and it soon became apparent that it required relocation. I jumped on this unexpected opportunity to extricate myself from my unhappy wife role. I asked for a divorce and left him behind in the Bay Area. Our disentanglement was an ugly fight over money but I only lost my coat, not my shirt.

## I Redeem Myself

After my divorce, I reverted to my serial monogamy pattern for several years, but no one even reached the spreadsheet stage in terms of marriage prospects.

Then one day when I was in the locker room at Equinox, an acquaintance approached me and told me there was a guy who wanted my email address. His name meant nothing to me so she told me the two things about him she deemed important: (1) he still has all his hair, and (2) I think he makes a good living. Those tidbits were not very helpful, but I'd seen this woman and a few of her friends working out with a man frequently and assumed he must be the guy.

The timing for a new relationship worked, as I had just dumped my latest beau. I scrawled my email address on a paper towel and handed it over. Apparently it was legible enough because he quickly did his homework and realized that we'd both attended Penn State. He tried to milk this commonality, expounding on his affection for the university and bragging up the fact that he still possessed primo football tickets. I'm sure he was sorely disappointed when he received my response informing him of my unhappy stint in Happy Valley and my disdain for the most watched spectator sport in the country.

Despite this misstep, we scheduled a coffee date for after work. At the last minute he canceled, claiming he had to work late. I assumed he'd gotten cold feet since it had taken him two years to muster the courage to even ask for my contact information. When I tried to reschedule for the weekend, he told me that he would be out of town at the Penn State football game.

But, as fate would have it, a hurricane barreled down the east coast that weekend and when I went to the gym on Saturday morning, I spotted him on one of the weight machines. I didn't pull any punches, greeting him with this snarky remark: "Well I see that you have at least a modicum of common sense."

Luckily, he took the comment in stride and we went upstairs to work out side-by-side on Stairmaster machines. While huffing and puffing our way through our routines, we got to know each other a bit and made dinner plans for that evening.

After our first meal together, my gut told me he was the guy I'd been looking for all this time. I know that sounds insane, especially coming from a hard-bitten cynical New Yorker. I'd heard of the soul mate thing but until Wes appeared in my life I'd given it about as much credence as winning the lottery or world peace breaking out. Right from the beginning we seemed to sync in so many ways and to share the same views on what really matters in life. We'd both been searching for someone who would make us a priority and we'd clearly found our respective matches.

Astoundingly, within 10 weeks we were married. I've rarely listened to my instincts, but in this instance I let my emotions prevail. I felt an unshakable certainty that Wes was the person I'd been looking for for so long to be my life partner. We've now been happily married for two decades and are hoping to eke out as many more years as we can get away with.

## Parting Thoughts

What I've learned is that you cannot redeem a bad marriage if you have chosen poorly. People are made out of stone, not clay. Before you say "I do," be darn sure. Don't settle for "good enough."

# | 6 |

## Lorie's Marital Advice #2

I know I'm being presumptuous offering this advice but perhaps I've picked up a few tidbits that some reader might be able to put to good use. Since I've just celebrated 20 wondrous years with my husband, I think I've earned the right to spew a bit of counsel, particularly having first endured seven years of marital hell.

The good news is that I have distilled my pearls of wisdom down to four simple points. My hope is that you might spot a gem that resonates with you.

### #1: Constant Nurturing is a Must

I've heard people say that marriage requires work, but I prefer to use the word "nurturing" because it connotes a more positive tone. Any relationship, especially an intimate one, requires a willingness to make compromises. When you decide to forsake singlehood you make a commitment to a union. You and your spouse have made a public statement that being able to do whatever your little heart desires whenever you want to will go by the wayside in order to cultivate a loving relationship with your worthy partner. Ignoring this basic reality and steadfastly clinging to your single ways will lead either to a roommate arrangement or to constant arguing. I experienced both the first time around.

My first marriage started poorly and slid downhill at the pace of an Olympic bobsledder. Neither of us strayed from our pre-marriage lifestyles one iota after we tied the knot. I continued to work like a crazy woman and Richard clung to his mama's boy role prioritizing her needs over mine.

The one area we actually tried to reach consensus on, divvying up the household chores, bombed out. We sat down and made a list of who would be responsible for the weekly tasks necessary to keep the household running smoothly. I thought I was being extremely magnanimous by agreeing to an even split of duties even though I worked many more hours than my husband clocked as a government employee. We worked through our list and I assumed it was all settled. I failed to realize that my husband had never been burdened with a household chore in his life and would find a way to avoid these unwelcome responsibilities. Most weekends Richard just didn't get around to trekking to Safeway with my grocery list in hand. Instead, he'd disappear to the beach and ride the waves on his boogie board while I seethed my way through the grocery store aisles feeling bitter and angry. It was becoming evident that even small lifestyle changes were not going to happen. Our marriage devolved into two disgruntled roommates sharing a house together.

When I married my dream guy Wes, I tried to apply some of the hard-earned lessons from my first disastrous alliance of the heart. I realized that I needed to devote some bandwidth to nurturing this budding relationship if I wanted it to flourish and create joy in my life.

Up to this point, my life and identity had consisted of living and breathing the practice of law. I thought the concept of work-life balance was a farce; a pipe dream totally beyond my capabilities. Since I'm a Type A+, I realized that I was incapable of being a part-time lawyer and that I needed to make a clean break and move on. I hoped that I would be able to pull off some version of work-life balance with a different choice.

So I took the leap and created head space to build a life for myself and my newfound soulmate. I did much better the second time out of the gate. The primary reason we enjoy peace and harmony at home is our willingness to engage in give-and-take in the spirit of generosity.

While it may sound like a trifling matter, my favorite part of each workday (I still have six) is sitting down to dinner with my husband and sharing our highlights and lowlights of the day. In order to enjoy that habit, we've committed to getting home by about 5:30 pm. Except for very rare circumstances, we make that happen. I leave the office even when I'd rather stay and finish something up and Wes drags himself off the golf course even when he's in the middle of a stellar round.

## #2: Do Not Keep Score

I know many couples who keep score of the concessions they have made to their spouses. They keep a running tally to ensure that they do not give up any more than they get. For example, if the wife puts up with her husband's family for Thanksgiving, she makes darn sure that they spend Christmas with her relatives, even if—having decided that he is not good enough for their darling—they treat her husband poorly. But tit for tat does not exactly create a convivial home environment.

Marriage #1 was filled with score-keeping on a par with the esoteric point system used to judge professional gymnastics meets. This was the type of exchange that would boil up during arguments:

Lorie: *Don't forget that I went to your family's all-day Thanksgiving dinner and choked down your mother's dried out turkey and tasteless stuffing.*

Richard: *First of all, don't you dare criticize my mother's cooking. And what about the Christmas gala you drag me to every year that requires me to put on a silly suit and listen to your legal buddies go on and on all night about their law cases? Do you think that's fun for me?*

Since there were far more of the time-consuming family get-togethers than there were law firm events, this perceived inequity led me to blow a gasket every time Richard attempted to impose an additional command performance.

Wes and I didn't approach our marriage as a score-keeping endeavor. Instead, we've tried to fulfill each other's needs and to err on the side of giving more than we get. I'm not sure how this shift occurred, but my attitude now is that it's my responsibility to do everything I can to create a marriage that serves as a comfortable refuge from the crazy world we live in today. I value "marital peace" first and foremost. A simple thing like texting a goofy gif each day goes a long way.

We both try to accommodate each other's obligations, whether related to our businesses, friends, or families. Luckily we're usually on the same page in terms of what events we'd like to attend and where we'd like to vacation. I guess attitude is everything. Our unselfish perspectives mean that we don't harbor unvoiced or unresolved resentments toward each other. That brings me to my next point.

### #3: Use an LED Light Not a Broom

Two people, no matter how compatible, will disagree from time to time, and sometimes those differences of opinion will be very strongly felt. One approach which I often employed with Richard was to just let things blow over without discussing them. I got into this unhealthy pattern after several failed attempts to start a civil discussion only to be met with a multi-day scream-fest followed by the silent treatment.

Having had The Bickersons for parents, I had no desire to live with that level of tension and hair-trigger tempers ever again. As a result, I swept many of our differences under the rug. Although I often went along with my husband's wishes, I harbored mega amounts of resentment and anger. That lingering bad taste made it hard for me to have an open, supportive relationship with my husband and occasionally even produced some passive aggressive behavior that I'm not very proud of.

It took me a while to see, but at some point in our marriage, it became glaringly obvious that Richard would always put his mother before me. He revered her in almost God-like terms and his level of commitment was to ask her how high to jump to satisfy her every whim. I, unfortunately, did not rate.

The role Richard had fully expected me to play as his wife, but neglected to mention to me until we got married, was to happily participate in all family gatherings, which entailed, at a minimum, eating dinner with his Mom twice a week. While his mother was a perfectly pleasant person, I had nothing in common with her and was unable to contribute to the endless discussions about all the fun times that were had when her husband was alive.

Initially I sucked it up like a good soldier and showed up at my mother-in-law's house for dinner as scheduled. Of course there were any number of additional family events for special occasions and holidays. Given my parsimonious spare time, I bridled under the expectation that I devote all of it to my husband's family. This feeling prevailed for the seven years of our marriage, mostly swept under the rug, but occasionally bursting forth into full-blown battle.

In contrast, due in large part to watching his parents engage in the pretense of never having any differences worthy of discussion, Wes never uses the broom approach. At the first sign that something is amiss, we turn on the LED lights and discuss it before our differences start to harden.

Conflict is an unavoidable part of any relationship. Unless you married your clone, from time to time there will inevitably be issues that require discussion and resolution. The key is to air your disagreements as soon as they arise, long before they assume exaggerated importance and disrupt your peace and harmony.

### #4: Keep Your Big Mouth Shut Now and Then

This last point is one that took me a long time to institute. When I married Wes I adopted the approach that I needed to tell him every little detail about everything. Perhaps I went to this extreme as an overreaction to keeping my lip buttoned up for so many years. Another driver for my over-sharing approach was likely my pent up need to share my thoughts with a husband who had a clue what I was talking about after having been deprived during my first marriage-go-round. I've since learned that I don't need to voice every thought that comes into my head and Wes doesn't need to hear every tiny particular to understand the big picture.

One area requiring reflection has been this: I have a tendency to vent about things that are frustrating me. My favorites at the moment are my chronic shoulder rotator cuff injury that never seems to heal and the fact that the phone does not ring as frequently as I'd like with prospective clients seeking my services.

Like night follows day, Wes will interpret my rant as a request for help and offer suggestions for resolution. My immediate reaction had been to dismiss each and every idea out of hand without even giving it a moment's consideration—likely because I never wanted any input in the first place. I just wanted to complain. I finally realized that he interprets my knee-jerk rebuff as perhaps a wee bit insulting. My self-analysis is that my bad behavior comes not from a desire to rebuff Wes' solutions or to make him feel like an idiot, but from a mindset that I am fully capable of solving my own problems and that's what I've always done.

After years of offending him, I've finally learned to take a breath, listen to his advice, and then at least agree to take it under submission.

Live and learn. I guess that's what life's all about.

# | 7 |

## Got Pain?

Many of us have experienced chronic pain. I must have been a particularly heinous person in a former life as I seem to have been dealt more than my fair share. Three prolonged periods of chronic pain feels a bit like overkill. But then again, no one asked my permission.

It's particularly unfair for a person like me, who does her best to model a healthy lifestyle, for the pain gods to have taken an unwarranted interest in me. How did I get so lucky? Did God want to teach me patience? If so, the lesson has failed to take.

If you're willing to suffer through my saga with me, you'll find some words of wisdom at the end of each episode.

### Episode #1: Abdominal Pain

For about 10 years I tolerated ever-increasing abdominal pain. It started out as really bad menstrual cramps that nagged at me all day for a few days a month pre-period, but progressively ramped up to about three weeks out of every four.

OTC pain relievers and heating pads proved useless. My GP tried one diagnostic test and drug after another including sonograms that showed no endometriosis, a colonoscopy that failed to reveal so much as a single polyp, a series of birth control pills, and an antidepressant. In desperation she suggested a very severe type of hormone therapy, which I researched and rejected based on the scary sounding side-effects.

Finally I got desperate enough to consider surgery to remove my unused girlie parts. The first surgeon counseled against it on the grounds that it seemed a bit extreme to do major surgery without a clear diagnosis. Dissatisfied with just one rejection, I went for a second consultation. Physician #2 asked probing questions about the quality of my life saddled with unrelenting pain and suggested that even though undergoing a complete hysterectomy might feel like a crazy desperation move, it might actually give me a pain-free life. The more I ruminated about it, the more I liked his logic. At least this treatment offered some possibility of permanent pain relief after enduring so many years in a perennially disgruntled crabby body.

I went ahead and had the operation despite the last minute curve ball the surgeon threw me the day before he cut. He told me that if he were me he would not have the hysterectomy since we had no assurance that it would rid me of the pain. I flippantly responded, "You haven't been living in this body," and proceeded to ignore him. As it turned out, I'd guessed right. The pain was obliterated forever and a normal life returned!

## Words of Wisdom

- Keep looking for a solution no matter how many wild goose chases you go on.
- Apply your own observational powers and logic rather than handing over the keys to the kingdom to the MDs.
- Choose the solution you think gives you the best quality of life.
- Once your pain issue is fully resolved, quickly put the episode behind you and return to your normal worries and aggravations.

## Episode #2: Nerve Pain

My next foray into debilitating pain was also quite lengthy. I endured an entire year of cry-worthy sharp pain in my left thigh. In addition to creating the need for a daily pity party, the intense throbbing prevented me from standing for more than about 2 minutes. Walking even a short distance such as from the parking lot to a store or restaurant was also a no-go. I came to dread shopping, particularly the interminable waits to check out. Many a time I had no choice but to squat down in the middle of the aisle to recover. My evening walks degenerated into hobbling from one fire hydrant to the next, resting at each to get the weight off my leg. My only respites were sitting and sleeping. I maintained some semblance of exercise by figuring out that my injured body was able to tolerate riding the recumbent bike and lifting upper body weights.

While it was readily apparent that putting weight on the leg was excruciatingly painful, the diagnosis was elusive and took me six months of digging. My health care practitioners were stumped. So I took to Google and just kept searching until one day "voila," I found a description that fit the bill.

As usual, I'd managed to become stricken with quite an unusual ailment. I had a damaged nerve, but not the usual sciatica in the back of the leg. That would be too pedestrian for my body. I'd managed to annoy the femoral nerve, which runs down the quad. Treatment consisted of waiting for time to pass to allow it to regrow and regenerate. This is an excruciatingly slow process like watching paint dry. So in the meantime I went to my physical therapist mainly to cry on his shoulder and find out what type of workouts I could get away with without setting back my recovery.

At some point I submitted to an MRI despite my claustrophobic fears. It showed that I had disc degradation that had likely led to trapping and squishing the femoral nerve. The test basically confirmed that we already knew—that the pain would not dissipate until the nerve fully regenerated. The damage could have been due to normal aging, but I took responsibility and assumed that it was triggered by my macho behavior of attempting to lift an excessive amount of weight while doing barbell squats.

In my case it took an entire year for the angry nerve to calm down and heal and in the meantime the pain stayed at the same consistently high level, which didn't do much for my morale. In retrospect, I feel sorry for my husband. While I am generally not a crybaby, I acted like one frequently during that time. There were many times I saw no light at the end of the tunnel and wanted to throw in the towel and give up on a return to a normal existence. My physical therapist told me that I was wrong and I tried hard to believe him. During the recovery process I ruined several vacations, including one to beautiful Maui, where the only activity I could engage in was reclining on the lanai chaise lounge with a good book. Excursions and waterfall hikes were not in the plan. It made for a less than exciting holiday for my long-suffering husband.

## Words of Wisdom

- People are so self-centered today that if you park your butt on the floor in a store aisle they will pretend you are invisible and certainly not bother to ask about your wellbeing.
- Pain makes me crabby, narcissistic, and less than scintillating to be around.
- Living with someone afflicted with chronic pain turns the home atmosphere into a real bummer.
- Never give up on your body no matter how intense the pain or how long it takes to see improvement.

## Episode #3: Shoulder Pain

This is my current fight. Over a year ago I ended up back in physical therapy as a result of abusing my body with too many injury/healing cycles from overhead lifting at the gym. Finally my left shoulder proclaimed "no more" with severe pain as the messenger. I'm left-handed so it was hard not to notice when the pain became constant.

I'll go into more detail in the next chapter about what caused this injury and how my Google search, my physical therapist's incorrect conclusion, and the eventual diagnosis by an orthopedic surgeon specializing in sports medicine took me on a long winding road of fruitless efforts to deal with the pain. But deal with it, I must. So I've adopted a certain amount of acceptance combined with patience, slowing down, and moving more thoughtfully. Currently, the pain rears its ugly head during so many normal activities of daily life that I try to use my right arm as much as possible, almost as if the injured one were in a sling. But some things like taking a shower and getting dressed and fixing my hair and face so I don't scare people off, are unavoidable and quite painful. Even using utensils with my left arm hurts, so I have taught myself to eat right-handed. Maybe it will save me from Alzheimer's. I've read that it's a good brain exercise to eat with your non-dominant hand.

## Words of Wisdom

- The body eventually heals itself, but in the meantime it's important to keep trying anything that might help and probably won't kill you, to keep yourself distracted.

- You will adjust to almost any type of limitation if you absolutely have to.
- Keep focusing on all of the things you still are capable of doing even if you have to fake your way through some of them.
- Keep your brain occupied so it doesn't have the luxury of focusing on how much your body hurts.

# | 8 |

## Lorie Gets Her Comeuppance

### Dealing with an Aging Body is No Fun

I'm 68 years old now, and despite my diligent efforts, my body is definitely talking to me a lot more than it used to. For the most part, it's complaining. I liked it better when it just performed as expected, without the repercussion of injury and pain. Now it insistently screams "Lorie, give your old body some respect and treat me with TLC if you want me to function properly." And it plaintively begs "Would you please lighten up on the macho weight workouts?"

I finally heard the pleas and begrudgingly incorporated daily stretching, going to an assisted stretch lab, getting regular massages (I know, no sympathy on that one), and adding balance training into my busy schedule. I feel like I devote extraordinary amounts of time babying my old carcass just to maintain a semi-healthy body not riddled with aches and pains or muscle tears and pulls. Apparently, this coddling is non-negotiable if I want this somewhat worn-out structure to be pain-free and fairly operational.

As a gerontologist, I know that bodies reach the height of their physical capabilities in order to procreate and then are designed to slowly wear out and wind down. The symptoms of this process include stiffness, tightness, achiness, a certain amount of pain, and vulnerability to injury. When you're as stubborn as I am about maintaining habits, acceding to these changes feels downright distressing. Even though I'm fond of saying that aging "beats the alternative," I keep trying desperately to deny reality and pretend I'm still a sexy looking 20-something. But then I get a glimpse in the mirror and receive a stark reminder that I've turned into that old lady.

## A Few Examples of My Pigheadedness

I talked about dealing with pain. Let me share just two examples of how my stubborn pigheadedness got me there. I've been lifting weights about five times a week for at least 40 years. When I strength train, I go into macho mode. Perhaps that's because I learned to build muscle from a former Mr. Universe (but that's another story). Nothing makes me happier than sitting down at a weight machine just vacated by a guy and upping the weight-load. I've indulged this ridiculous head trip to the point of injury.

In the last chapter, I recounted the year-long saga of injury, diagnosis, and eventual healing of excruciating nerve pain in my leg. Here's how it happened. One time I was at the Smith machine and I noticed a buff woman next to me doing squats with a heavily weighted barbell on her shoulder. I decided there was no reason that I couldn't match her pound for pound. Somehow the fact that she was about half my age and almost twice my weight failed to register.

On the third squat, I felt a sharp pain in my back. I later discovered that the discs in my back had moved and managed to trap my femoral nerve. Pigheadedness was definitely the culprit in this instance. It took an entire year and dozens of sessions of physical therapy to regenerate the nerve. The myriad ways in which this pain limited my mobility, interfered with daily life, and ruined what would have otherwise been wonderful vacations must be taken to heart. Perhaps being a bit more realistic along with a healthy dose of common sense would have saved me—I can now say in hindsight.

## My Latest Attempt to Deny Aging and Stay in Control

Here are the gory details (alluded to above) of how stubborn denial got me into another episode of trouble. Apparently decades of overhead shoulder presses have taken a toll on my body. Go figure! On some level, I knew that I'd pay for the repeated cycles of injury, rest, and repair. This pattern should have been a wake-up call that I was pushing my body beyond its limits. But no; I ignored it. I had buff shoulders and arms that made me feel strong, so I persisted until the injury phase became my permanent condition.

At that point, my left shoulder couldn't take the abuse anymore and suddenly I was experiencing pain while doing normal things like lifting my arm overhead trying to take off a dress or shirt. I also noticed a constant dull throbbing emanating from my shoulder that radiated down to my elbow. That got my attention to the point where I called my GP and asked for a physical therapy referral.

The therapist initially suggested an X-ray or an MRI, both of which I rejected out of hand. Google had already told me I had the classic symptoms of a rotator cuff tear and the therapist agreed. So, what was the point of an unnecessary test, especially one that would bring on a claustrophobic panic attack? The clinician gave me an ever-increasing list of exercises designed to improve my range of motion and strength to perform both in his office and at home.

For several months that treatment appeared to be effective and then the progress stalled. My husband kept telling me to give up on PT and try something else, but I persisted for a total of 10 months at which point I mysteriously got worse to the point of experiencing throbbing pain that woke me up in the middle of the night. My solution was to attack that problem with sleep remedies ranging from Blue Ice, to CBD cream, to a topical NSAID, to Tylenol PM, to melatonin. Nothing worked.

I finally got desperate enough to agree to an MRI. I opted for the "open" version and was able to get though it without wriggling out of the machine and bolting from the room. When I got the results, I learned that I had a much different problem than the one the therapist had been trying to treat.

It turns out that I have severe arthritis in my left shoulder, along with quite a few inflamed tendons. So, I went off to a well-qualified sports medicine physician and let him talk me into a steroid injection. That was an aberration for me because I hate putting drugs of any kind in my body and steroids are seriously powerful. But it seemed like an intelligent choice and the constant pain had me in a worn down state.

As it turned out, I learned that I have a body which is just as unique as my personality. My body went into an over-reactive mode and tightened up even more in reaction to the injected remedy, which served to increase the pain and decrease the range of motion. Not the hoped-for result. So that was a failed experiment. Logic leads me to believe that the degraded joint is not the source of the pain, but that I have a repetitive stress injury caused by 40+ years of overhead lifts.

Next up is a second opinion from another sports medicine physician and a resumption of physical therapy. At this point, I'd be a happy camper just to be back to the pre-injection pain level. Oy vey, as we Jews like to say. (If you're wondering how this Jewish girl ended up in Catholic school being taught by nuns, well just read on. Most parents keep secrets from their kids and mine did too. This one, which I didn't learn of until I was in my 50s, was a doozy!)

I'd say I got my comeuppance. Maybe it's time to ease up a bit on this old body and adopt some new patterns that fit my stage in life a bit better. What do you think?

# | 9 |

## Life Throws Lorie a Curve Ball

I spent quite a bit of time whining about my chronic shoulder pain. Guess what? God/he/she/it/whatever/whoever decided that I needed to be distracted. That certainly stopped my laser focus on upper body pain.

### And I Thought Walks Were Boring

I've never been much on walking. I've tried Spotify, podcasts, listening to stand-up, and texting everyone I know, and walking still bores me. I'd rather just take off running and get back to the starting gate. The only thing that helps is having someone, preferably my loving husband, come along so we can talk. Then my brain is elsewhere.

But since I sit on my butt all day I know I need to get my body moving before it atrophies in place. So every day I go for a one-mile walk around the Crossroads Shopping Center across the street from my office. It's short enough to feel doable.

One Friday, I was doing my usual walk and waited the requisite 3 minutes until the generic walking human icon gave me permission to cross the street. I made it safely to the turn lane when I noticed a small orange car traveling at an excessive rate of speed. When the driver saw me she slammed on the brakes, but by that time, I was most of the way through the crosswalk. I made eye contact with her, lifting my hands up in the universal WFT motion. I then proceeded to cross behind her car since it was way past the crosswalk.

Suddenly, for reasons that elude logic, she put the car in reverse and the next thing I knew, I was on the ground with my legs pinned under a car tire. I immediately realized that this was not going to be a good day. Instead of helping clients with their health, I'd be checking in for an extended stay at the ER.

## There are Still Kind People Out There

Despite being bloodied up and screaming in pain, I was immediately heartened by the kindness of strangers. Someone called 911 while others hoisted me out of the street and gingerly deposited me on the sidewalk. I heard a chorus of "How can I help?" entreaties. One of the witnesses was an RN who correctly triaged the laceration as being down to the ankle bone. That didn't sound good.

Another kind soul went back to her car and got a bottle of water for me. A big beefy guy was so irate that he went after the runner-overer who had fled the scene. He proudly returned to report that he had tracked her down.

Within a few minutes I was creating a major traffic jam as a fire truck, ambulance, and what seemed like every police car in the City of Irvine, converged at the intersection. Meanwhile I had voice texted my husband and later learned that my message was bizarrely conveyed like this:

> Somebody just have me on the street call Vern Baranco
> please from sweetheart rollaway.

I obviously had pressed "send" without proofreading the word salad Siri wrote. What I meant to say was a bit different:

> Somebody just hit me on the street at Culver and Barranca.
> Please come sweetheart. Right away.

When Scottie failed to beam my husband to the scene immediately, I called him and explained the situation in English. Once he had a comprehensible message, he drove to the scene as fast as he could. As soon as I saw him, I took a deep breath for the first time since being run over and felt comforted.

As I was being peppered with a chorus of questions from the first responders, I noticed out of the corner of my eye that several of the witnesses had stuck around to give police reports. Chalk up another one to the kindness of strangers.

## Off to Hoag Hospital for Treatment

Next, I was carted away in the ambulance to Hoag Hospital, answering questions all the way and having my vitals taken over and over. Once I arrived, I was taken into a cubicle and asked to repeat the narrative many more times.

Everyone who tended to my care for the next four hours was very empathetic. They all called me "dear," which was quite comforting. The attending looked like McDreamy on *Grey's Anatomy*. I wasn't complaining.

It took some time for the portable X-ray machine to be wheeled in to confirm that there was no fracture in my ankle. That was a huge relief and allowed me to later make the snarky remark to my GP that a bone density test would not be necessary this year.

My body became a pin cushion for injections of tetanus, pain medication, and a double dose of heavy duty antibiotics. Finally the PA stitched me up and I was on my way.

## The Aftermath

Once I had been escorted out pushing my brand new and wholly superfluous walker, I decided I was quite capable of going back to my office to keep my existing 4:00 pm appointment. The client was about to embark on a Disney Cruise and needed some help planning healthy meals. After keeping that appointment, I prepped for the next day and drove myself home as usual.

I ate dinner with my husband while trying to make sense of the day and then we went on our usual after-dinner walk with my mummified leg. I was so numbed and drugged up that I was feeling no pain. After half watching my usual cooking and home remodel shows, I gingerly climbed into bed vainly hoping to sleep through the night. Not so fast! Pain issued a wake-up call in the middle of the night, so I quickly downed a Percodan and eventually got back to sleep.

I took another Percodan in the morning to keep ahead of the pain, did a short walk, and went to work. I was feeling proud of myself as I got through the day until another curve ball came whizzing past. Out of the blue, the room started spinning and I became nauseous. Somehow I faked my way through my last 2 appointments. Sometimes the side effects are worse than the pain. No more Percodan for me.

I hobbled through the weekend and on Monday, was able to get in to see my primary care physician, who is wonderful. Naturally, she gave me after-care instructions that were 180 degrees different from Dr. McDreamy's. I chose to go with her, more current, regimen.

One week after the incident I was able to slowly get back to my life with some semblance of normalcy, testing the waters on resuming minimal workouts to help get the blood moving and the lymph moving out. I felt like a leaky faucet and was convinced that my legs were transplanted from a 95 year-old sedentary diabetic. Not my favorite look.

## Not Making Lemonade, But on the Mend

I'm nowhere near noble enough to make lemonade from lemons, plus it would never be my beverage of choice. But there certainly are some reasons to feel gratitude.

- My husband was a saint and the incident has brought us closer together.
- The unbroken ankle bone allowed me to pat myself on the back for working out.
- I escaped with just a nasty looking scar on my ankle.
- I preferred my position to that of the woman who hit me.
- I became an expert in effective wound care.
- I got a surfeit of love and support from friends and clients.
- I'm a lot more careful as a driver and pedestrian.
- The ordeal helped me appreciate normal life more.

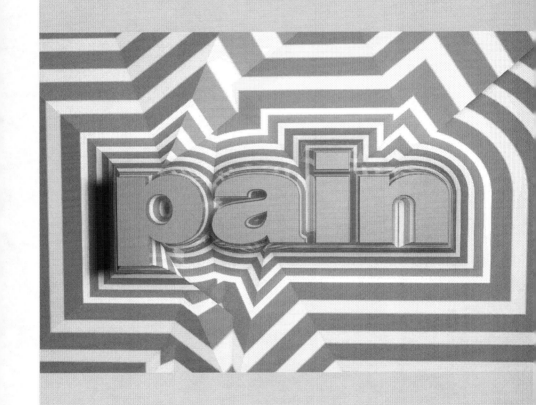

# | 10 |

## More About Pain

Before I turn to more cheery health topics, I want to share a bit more about the aftermath of the hit and run. I experienced a prolonged ordeal with the pain devil. So please indulge me in a little navel-gazing about my journey into the netherworld.

### My Unexpectedly Painful Road to Recovery

Until I lived through this trauma, I was naïve about how intense pain can be. No more. As it turned out, I had to face the full force of the searing pain unassisted by pharmaceuticals. My body responded to Percodan by transforming my office into a nauseating amusement park ride that I never wanted take. A weaker opioid only served to cast a shroud over me to the point that I was nodding off during my 15 minute commute to the office. The fog persisted until mid-afternoon and then exhaustion set in.

Within a few days, the all-encompassing nature of the pain became as undeniable as the fact that bad things sometimes happen to good people. I used to think that the persistent ache of my rotator cuff injury was bad, but a deep ankle laceration, in combination with extensive areas of raw skin wounds, presented a dimension of agony I had never experienced in my life.

Without getting overly dramatic, the level of unrelenting, all-consuming acute pain I experienced prevented me from holding a cogent thought. The only short respites occurred when I did my coaching and was forced to focus on another human being for half an hour.

I found it interesting to observe that the shoulder pain that had been the bane of my existence, seemed to go into remission because the leg pain trumped it temporarily. This syndrome of your brain only being able to focus on the most severe pain is one of nature's gifts.

While I definitely felt the need for a reward for enduring the undeserved agony, my indulgence of choice, a massage, was not feasible. Any normal person living with the shock and distress of this horrible episode would have stopped into Paris Baguette™ (which happens to be on my daily walking route), and binged on delectable treats. But since I'm not normal, that did not tempt me. Instead, I abused coffee as much as I could. And since I'm caffeine immune, the over-indulgence didn't even make me an Energizer bunny.

Keeping my extensive wounds clean, protected, and moist became quite a project. We set up wound care central in our kitchen and stocked it with silicone tape, non-stick pads, steri-strips, and a myriad of shapes and sizes of bandages. As my husband exhausted the supplies at one drug store, he hunted down other CVS™ locations.

I will probably be tagged on Amazon for abusing their return policy given how many shoe styles in various lengths and widths I ordered and returned trying to find one that would accommodate my bulging feet which looked like sausages ready to burst their casings.

## Top 10 Lessons Learned From the Pain Devil

Since I tend to be introspective, I want to share the top ten lessons I've learned from living in Hades.

1. I Became a Self-Absorbed Taker.

   Coping with this level of agony does not leave any room for thoughts about other people except to the extent that they can help you. There is no room for relationships when you are in that place.

2. I Hate Being Dependent.

   I am very self-reliant and like to do everything myself. Suddenly having to lean on my husband for both physical and emotional succor did not mesh well with my independent streak.

3. My Whole Body Was In an Upheaval.

The insult was not confined to the left leg that was crushed under the car tire. Surprisingly, my whole body swelled up. The fluid build-up was confirmed when 6 extra pounds registered on my scale. My GI system felt like the inside of the nutribullet constantly churning a smoothie. I turned into a gasping mouth-breather.

4. 15 Minute Chunks Are the Way to Go.

   My best strategy for getting through the day was to take it in 15 minute chunks. That approach prevented me from engaging in endless crying jags and over-indulging my "What did I do the deserve this?" feeling.

5. Brain Distraction Helps Tremendously.

   It never even occurred to me to stay home, lounge around, and feel sorry for myself. I chose to drag myself into work looking like James Stewart in the movie Rear Window. Of course, my appearance required me to tell my sorry tale to each client. But doing my job gave me purpose and a temporary respite from pain.

6. Mental Health Matters Too.

   For decades I have started each day with a strenuous workout. This habit is so long-standing that if I miss a day, I walk around mimicking the affect of the pitiful Charley Brown. Maintaining some form of body movement felt non-negotiable. So I found ways to keep up with my daily workouts, but had to ratchet them down to lame, faker sessions.

7. Reach Out When Wounded.

   I found myself attempting to elicit support from any anyone who might be willing to express sympathy, even observant strangers who noticed my copious bandages. I refused to suffer in silence. I wanted the world to know my pain and greedily soaked up any solicitude that came my way.

8. Mini-Pity Parties Help.

   I permitted myself a daily mini-pity party. That kept me from being constantly self-absorbed and weepy. Because I would not be deterred from my shopping center loop walking route, I had to revisit the scene of the crime daily. I selected a sidewalk stretch on the way back to my office for a one-minute cry. It helped relieve the built-up angst and kept random tearing to a minimum.

9. Pain Can Fall Off a Cliff.

   I endured level 20 (on a scale of 1-10) pain for three weeks straight with no relief in sight. The worst part of the day was the transition from lying in bed to standing up. The first attempts at weight bearing hurt so much that it was all I could do not to howl like a mortally wounded animal. Then one day when I carefully tried to stand upright, the level of pain was significantly less to the point where I could almost contemplate immediately descending the staircase to get to my beloved coffee, rather than practice-walking for five minutes before gingerly hopping down the stairs clutching the banister for dear life.

10. The Smell of Lymph is Nauseating.

    The production of white blood cells called lymph fluid is the body's way of healing wounds. It's a good thing. For several weeks the wounds were leaching such copious amounts that I felt like a leaky faucet. This fluid had a definite stench to it. After several days of wound care and extensive bandage replacement, I came to dread that nasty stench just as much as the pain of ripping off the stained coverings.

## Now I Have Another Job

Healing aside, I have a brand new job that will probably require my time and attention for the next year. Now I get to wrangle with two insurers and Medicare to get my bills paid and obtain some compensation for this misadventure.

After finally wresting a copy of the police report out of the Irvine P.D., I discovered that the hit-and-runner only had $10,000 of liability coverage because she qualified for a low income, low-limits policy. That won't go far. So I have to exhaust that policy and then haggle with my insurance company to prove entitlement under the under-insured motorist's coverage. And finally, I have the privilege of dealing with the government bureaucracy called Medicare.

It will be a long and winding road navigating this laborious claims process and I will likely not feel fully recompensed at the end. Many have advised me to sue, but I don't see any percentage in going that route. I have no desire to relive the experience in court, and the hit-and-runner is an 80-year old with no money. There's no point in obtaining an uncollectible judgment. The best I can hope for is that the imposition of a point on her license and being kicked out of the low-limits program will make it prohibitively expensive for her to continue to be a danger on the road.

## Take-Away from Pain Experience

Constant searing pain is debilitating, physically and mentally. It is so consuming that it's darn near impossible to entertain cognitive thought. If I'm ever in this much pain again, I want to be taken out back and shot immediately. Perhaps I can add an Addendum to my Advance Health Directive. Kidding, not kidding...

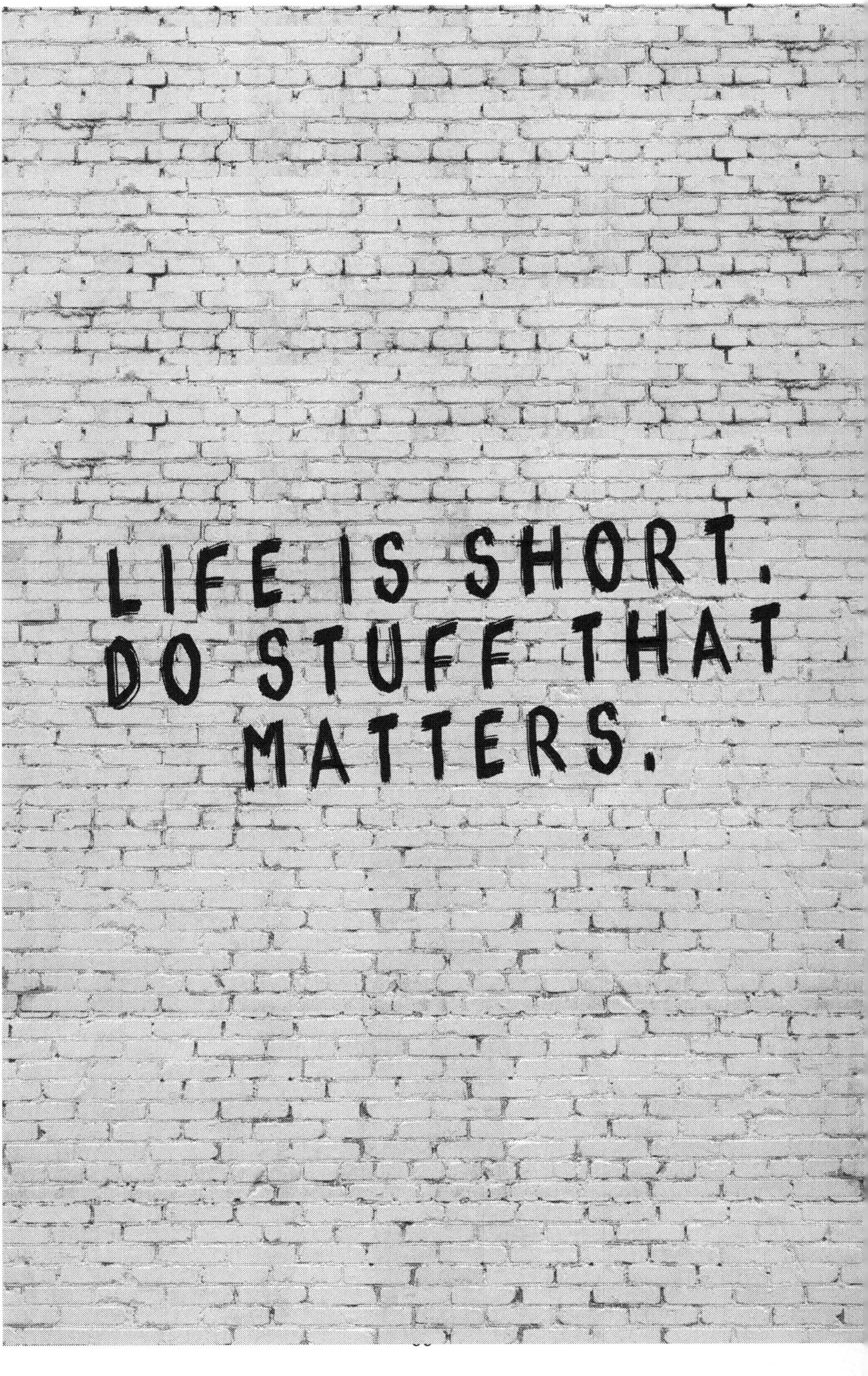
LIFE IS SHORT.
DO STUFF THAT
MATTERS.

# | 11 |

## Life Lessons from Running My Business

I started my wellness coaching business 10 years ago and somehow managed to create a thriving enterprise. My trajectory definitely did not follow the *Field of Dreams* "build it and they will come" fantasy. When I hear entrepreneurs claim that their businesses "just blew up," I jealously assume they are lying. Real life is more often like J.K. Rowling's experience of having her wildly successful Harry Potter book rejected by 12 publishers before finally being picked up by an editor who advised her to keep her day job.

Part of the reason I beat the odds and did not crash and burn is simply that I am one stubborn individual. I refuse to give up. If one avenue leads to a dead end, I choose another. It occurred to me that the attributes needed to nurture a business and keep it thriving teach valuable lessons that can be applied more broadly to life. Here are five that I want to share with you:

### Lesson #1: Choose a Life That Gives You Purpose and Brings Joy.

If I had not chosen to focus my business on my passion for making the world healthier one person at a time, my fledgling enterprise would have dried up and blown away like a spent dandelion in no time. As soon as I hung out my shingle, to borrow from legal slang, it became apparent that in typical Lorie fashion, I'd chosen the most challenging niche of the healthy nutrition weight loss business and that this would be a bumpy ride.

While most people want to live a healthier lifestyle, which usually means losing weight and getting into a consistent exercise routine, they are impatient. Once they decide they want to shoehorn themselves into their skinny jeans, they want the fat cells to miraculously and instantaneously evaporate like water on hot pavement.

New ways to do this with yet another miracle diet constantly show up on social media. Now Ozempic and Zepbound are all the rage and big pharma is racing to develop new versions of these drugs that promise even more dramatic weight loss. The drug companies are making a mint and downplaying the fact that their users will inevitably regain the weight as soon as they stop paying $1,000 a month for the injectable. Yet demand is outstripping supply, a testament to the fact that people are willing to bear the astronomical cost and put up with the sometimes severe side effects to get the speedy results they yearn for.

Since I do not promise instantaneous results, I just have to work harder than the competition to get noticed on the Internet and find clients who know that "if it sounds too good to be true, it probably is."

Summary: Choose the life that makes you happy and start living it. Resist the temptation to go through life putting in time at a job you hate, counting the days to retirement, or toughing it out in a moribund relationship. Don't settle for good enough. Aim for the best life that you can achieve. It's worth putting in the work to get what you want. Unless you're betting on reincarnation, there are no second chances.

## Lesson #2: Get Comfortable Making Decisions with Incomplete Information.

I am not like my husband who bravely jumps in with both feet and then cleans up the debris later. My mindset is that of a logical lawyer who spends an inordinate amount of time gathering all pertinent information and then carefully evaluates it from every possible angle before putting one toe in the water.

If you want to start a business, get comfortable doing a high dive off a cliff. You have to get over your trepidation and move forward knowing that you don't really have much of a clue about what you're doing or whether it will work. You can spend years learning about your competition, networking with possible cross-referral sources, and talking to people in need of your services. I did some of this but after delaying probably far too long, I held my breath, bravely jumped into the deep end, and start swimming. There was quite a bit of splashing and flailing around until I derived a sustainable business model to get my new career off the ground, but I did it.

Summary: We tend to put off difficult things because we get overwhelmed by the choices or are afraid to make the wrong decision. The result is that we do nothing, which is actually a decision by default. If you have a dream in life, make it happen and enjoy the journey. Don't die with regrets.

## Lesson #3: Force Yourself To Be Incompetent.

After 23 years of practicing law I was feeling very competent and secure in my career. But try as I might, I could no longer ignore that creeping "been there, done that" feeling that was beginning to seep in to my being. I was no longer champing at the bit to get to the office and felt less engaged in my cases. That unease, along with a fear that I would ruin marriage #2, forced me to think deeply about where I was in my life at age 49.

As thoughts of retiring from the practice started to take hold, I came to the conclusion that my marriage to my new husband would bring me far more joy than continuing to devote my life to being a hot shot litigator. So I bit the bullet and retired with no plan about a future career other than the certainty that I'd find one. It was scary and I spent a lot of time trying new avenues, working under 20 year-olds, and floundering around like a seal on dry land.

Summary: Use the well-worn phrase "get out of your comfort zone" if you must, but evaluate where you are in life and figure out how to make it better. Challenge yourself to do new things you are incompetent at and find new skills and talents to develop. You just might experience some magic you never expected.

## Lesson #4: Don't Rely on Experts to Solve Your Problems.

I've had my share of low points with my wellness coaching business. Covid was a gut punch, then inflation hit, and now weight loss injectables are creating new challenges for me. Every business owner struggles from time to time. It's easy to get discouraged when the flow of emails and texts from prospects slows to a trickle. When that happens, it's very tempting to troll the net for big name business gurus, listen to popular webinars, or spend a small fortune hiring consultants. I'm guilty of the latter. I've succumbed in weak moments and latched onto PR and social media experts to save me. Once I hired a very experienced marketing consultant who was confident she had the secret sauce to vastly expand my customer base. After six months I had zero additional prospects and a lighter bank account.

I also invested in Facebook, Google, and Yelp ads. The first two bombed out like the New Diet Coke and the third worked for a while and then became a bust as well. But I didn't stop there. In a moment of panic, I plopped down an embarrassingly large amount of money on a search engine optimization genius who promised me I would pop up in web searches as the primo nutritionist and weight loss coach in Orange County. The end product she delivered was a six page laundry list of "keywords" that I was instructed to use in all of my posts. Despite my efforts to liberally sprinkle those magic words like so much fairy dust, I did not see any appreciable increase in business.

Finally, after so many fruitless efforts, I've accepted the reality that I know my business better than anyone else ever will and plodding away with my own trial and error is the way to go.

Summary: Let your common sense, life experience, and intuition be your guides. Bite the bullet and make your own decisions and take responsibility for the results. Learn to trust your gut. It's usually right. Of course, you will make mistakes, but at least you will control your own destiny.

## Lesson #5: Cop to Mistakes and Treat Everyone Fairly.

Everyone makes mistakes. As long as you fess up and apologize you will always be forgiven. I'm not sure where customer service went, but these days it seems that only Zappos and Amazon "get it."

I firmly believe that keeping customers happy is one of the most important components of a successful business. In my work the customer is always right. I strive to figure out a way to make things work best for my clients.

For example, my Achilles heel is calendaring appointments. After all, there are just so many ways to mess up the days and times, especially since my clients change them all the time. And then there's the additional possibility of my forgetting to press save after entering a meeting time. My excuse is that I use a Google calendar on my Apple phone and they don't play well together. What often saves me is that I send reminders the day before and that unearths most of my errors before I end up embarrassing myself and have to fall on my sword.

Even when I know that the client made the mistake, I never point the finger at them. There's just no upside in doing so. I want to spread good will and make our interactions pleasant experiences that clients look forward to. I also pride myself on the personal attention I provide, which includes checking in with them during the week to provide any support they might need.

Summary: When you make an error, own it. Don't blame circumstances or other people for your failings. There's no harm in admitting that you're not God and that you made a mistake. What you learn is that the confessions of weakness often strengthen relationships.

You can't go wrong if you treat everyone the way you would like to be treated. There's no downside to being kind and thoughtful. If you're having a down day, say a kind word to someone, hold the door for them, or lend a sympathetic ear and you will get an emotional lift.

# | 12 |

## I'm Running as Fast as I Can

Do you feel like you're racing through life, just trying to make sure none of your spinning plates crash to the ground and break into a million pieces so that you have to corral the shards into a dustpan while desperately trying to avoid ending up in urgent care with a gusher?

I can relate. I have felt that way much of my life. When I practiced law, I shied away from drinking fluids because I didn't want the interruption of having to run to the restroom. Lunch only happened when I could no longer ignore my gnawing hunger cramps. Then I'd make a mad dash to the nearest grab-and-go shop for a tasteless turkey sandwich wrapped in Saran Wrap™ and scarf it down while I continued working. On Sunday, the one day I dared to take off from work, I'd cram in all my household and personal chores.

Downtime? Jews don't do that. Work life balance? Huh? My sole focus was to be the best lawyer I was capable of being so that I could break through the glass ceiling and achieve my life's mission of becoming a partner. I had such a laser focus that I just kept running as fast as I could to get to the prize. But even after I made partner, the craziness continued. I was saddled with more responsibilities than ever and then this over-achiever volunteered to open and manage a new office in SoCal.

I know I'm not alone. Most of us feel like the proverbial hamster on a wheel, never quite able to generate enough speed to get ahead in our own lives. It seems that our to-do lists are forever getting longer, causing a commensurate jump in our stress levels.

What's going on? I have some theories, which may or may not have any validity, and then I'll share my personal struggles at attempting to get off the hurtling Japanese bullet train and downshift to Amtrak.

## Sky-High Expectations

In every area of our lives, the demands on our time are escalating. This is particularly evident in the realms of parental and job responsibilities.

## Amped Up Parental Expectations

I realize that most of you have assumed much more serious obligations in life than I've ever attempted. Given my one-track life, I decided early on that motherhood was not in the cards both because I had no desire to outsource child raising and because I feared I would be as inadequate a mother as the one who raised me.

It sure seems like when I was a kid, parenting was less all-consuming than it is today. Most moms I knew enjoyed the financial luxury of not having to work. Their job was to raise their kids. Husbands were expected to bring home the bacon, but not to pitch in with mundane household duties or sneak out early to coach their kids' soccer teams.

Parents did not hover over their Jacks and Jills like helicopters to shield them from any and all negative life experiences. It was not considered bad parenting if your child fell down on the playground, skinned a knee, and started screaming like a banshee. If another kid teased your child, it was not immediately labeled "bullying" and brought to the attention of the appropriate authorities.

But today, women are expected to be multi-tasking perfectionists who adroitly juggle their full time jobs with their Super Mom responsibilities which include calming screaming infants, showing up at the office sleep deprived, wrangling their older kids off their phones at night to get them to do their homework, and operating a complimentary chauffeur service for their teenagers.

Men have ill-defined parental roles. Are they supposed to get up in the middle of the night when the baby cries? Change diapers? Drop off and pick up the kids at school? Spend all weekend at their daughter's volleyball games? Cook dinner? These are all issues that have to be worked out within each marriage and can lead to bitterness and resentment if they are not amicably resolved.

## Work is 24/7

We are always on the clock today. Most of us check our phones for new text messages first thing in the morning, effectively starting our workdays before we even leave the house. And while some of us are just compulsive, in most workplaces there is an unspoken expectation that employees can be reached after what we used to consider normal working hours. Since we want to be good employees and keep our jobs, we willingly comply.

Even when we are attempting to relax on a sunny beach in Maui or luxuriating in the spectacular blue waters of the Caribbean, we are not immune from work pressures. Despite our physical absence from the office, our indispensable phones keep us tethered to our jobs.

We reflexively check our work messages, if only to avoid returning to a backlog of 300 emails. And unfortunately, there are a diminishing number of locales where we can credibly claim to be off the grid. A decade or so ago we were able to take real vacations.

## New Life Stressors

Add in these additional concerns and it's easy to understand why we've all turned into stress messes. Technology and social networking are the biggest culprits, while worries about personal and cyber safety haunt us all the time.

## Technology

Technology, like the federal deficit, is totally out of control and it's only going to get worse. If things weren't crazy enough, artificial intelligence has now entered the fray, creating all kinds of new ethical issues for us to grapple with.

We are allowing the cyber world to rule our lives. I break into a sweat if I leave my phone at home or, God forbid, misplace it. I simply can't function. Many of us are now saddled with a double dose: a work phone and a personal phone. I have a religious friend who vowed to leave her phone in the car during Mass to show respect for God, but she couldn't pull it off. In the middle of the liturgy, she bolted out of the church to make sure she hadn't missed anything and was left with a feeling of shame.

Americans check their phones an appalling 144 times per day and I'm as guilty as the next person. I somehow feel compelled to respond instantaneously to a text from a client or prospective client just because I can. One of the easiest ways to grab a quick break is to watch Instagram or TikTok videos. Many of us get so enthralled scrolling social media sites that we cheat ourselves out of restful sleep. Our phones are on our nightstands within arm's reach, just in case.

This deep intrusion of tech into my life has definitely made me feel constantly anxious and even a bit out of control. I hear tell that the answer is to do a digital detox and surrender my trusty lifeline. I know some of you have successfully done that, but even the thought of attempting to do so makes me nervous. What if there is an emergency? What if I ignore a client or a prospect? My excuse is that I run my own small business. I'm sure you have an equally legitimate justification worked out.

## The World Feels Unsafe

When I was growing up in the DC burbs, it was normal for kids to be sent outside to play all day and only called back in with the dinner bell. Parents had no fear for their children's safety and neighbors looked out for each other. If I had kids today, I'd worry about their safety as soon as they left the house.

When I was in the fifth grade, we moved to New York City, where I walked everywhere without worrying about anything more serious than annoying catcalls from bored construction workers. Most of my friends lived in Queens so I rode the subways at all hours, exercising a little caution but never being in fear for my life.

Now I don't feel so safe, especially after our rental car was broken into near the Oakland Airport when we ran into the Mini-Mart to buy a bottle of water. That was enough time for thieves to bash the passenger window and abscond with my purse and phone containing all of my personal information. Our vacation went down in flames and I spent months remedying the damage, including changing my passwords on every site and securing new credit cards.

Encountering homeless people living on the streets has become normal. And while I pity them, I steer clear of them lest they do something crazy that jeopardizes my safety.

The news media exacerbates our fears by constantly hyping the violence in our society. Local news reporting consists of the daily tally of shootings, hit & run accidents, and street racing fatalities. It makes you wonder if there is anything positive happening in today's world.

Cybercrime is another big worry. My website has been hacked twice and both times I whipped myself into a frenzy worrying about my livelihood until it was recovered. It's now commonplace to receive notifications of suspicious charges on your credit card and have to close the account and get a new one. The term virus used to refer to bodily infections, but now denotes the havoc scammers cause targeting innocent computer users.

## My Life Adjustment to Slow
## My Exhausting Sprint to a Jog

So what can we do to get our priorities back in order and take control of our lives again?

When clients want stress reduction techniques, I suggest things like meditation, journaling, massages, mani-pedis, walking on the beach, listening to music, or binging on trashy Netflix series.

While these are all great ideas, in my case, I needed a much bigger adjustment. I've told you about my radical career shift almost 20 years ago when I retired from a 23-year career as a corporate litigator. I hadn't planned on that. But then my soulmate Wes showed up and we said "I do." That's when the status quo became unexpectedly unacceptable.

My new husband started doling out daily reprimands letting me know that I was ordering him around like he was my secretary. Oops. I guess I was supposed to be capable of transforming into a loving wife the moment I set foot in our house. For about six months I tried and failed miserably to pull off this magic trick, finally realizing that my only hope of creating a happy marriage was to make a clean break from my career.

Having made the decision, I realized that the undeserved societal respect for my chosen career as a lawyer was about to disappear. But what made me more uneasy was the idea that I would no longer be self-supporting. My mother had warned me about being dependent on a man.

Resigning turned out to be the easy part. The aftermath was unsettling and downright scary. My entire sense of myself consisted of my "Lorie the Lawyer" tough guy façade and I wasn't too sure if there was any other version of me underneath. But it was high time to find out.

In a single day I went from people constantly hounding me, demanding snippets of my time, to bouncing around an empty house feeling panicked that no one needed me and that I'd lost all sense of purpose. After I forced myself to calm down, I tentatively started on what turned out to be an extremely fulfilling journey of self-discovery. It was not a smooth path. Overwhelming feelings of anxiety sometimes intruded. In retrospect I would have benefited from talking to a psychologist, but of course Lorie thinks she can do everything on her own.

The transition was far from seamless. It was more like a series of fits and starts through various careers and lasted close to 10 years. But it was fun to finally permit my non-lawyer skills to see the light of day. At the end of the long and winding road lay my passion—helping people improve their health through wellness coaching.

Maybe there's something you can do to lessen your stress. You need not be as dramatic as I was. Even small snippets of relaxation help.

DO IT
BECAUSE
THEY
SAID
YOU
COULDN'T

# | 13 |

# How Did I Get to Be So Old So Fast?

I've been wanting to write about the subject of aging for some time but have delayed putting fingers to keyboard, as I've struggled to find a positive spin on getting old. During my time in the elder care field, I came up with this pithy saying to describe my idea of the optimal aging process: "healthy, healthy, healthy, healthy, dead."

The reality is that no one gets out alive. But we're all in the dark about how many more years we have left, so I keep my focus on the quality over the quantity. I want to feel good every day. I care very little about how many decades I'm on this planet before my soul goes wherever such things go. And you never know, maybe I'll hang around more than 122 years and set a new longevity record.

## Coping with the Aging Process

It seems like I blinked and now I'm an old lady, being called "Ma'am" by the ever-shrinking minority of younger people who still respect their elders. Since healthy living is my career focus, I have more incentive than most to stay healthy. All things considered, I'm hanging in there pretty well, especially compared to some of my contemporaries.

Coping with aging is both a physical and mental chore and one in which every day is a new adventure. Some days I just feel like everything is going to hell in a hand basket, to use a dated expression. I wake up and realize that a new and different body part is behaving badly and then I start obsessing about whether this is going to be a permanent issue in my life, or worse yet, whether it portends something fatal. I always hope that I'll dodge the bullet and the problem will magically disappear overnight. Often it does. But in the meantime, I worry. A lot.

On other days, when I'm in my cycling class riding next to a 20-something who is dogging it while I'm barely winded, I'm floating on cloud nine. If only I weren't such a realist, I could savor the feeling longer. Instead, a quick reality check tells me she either partied all night and has a splitting headache or has clipped into her pedals with a mere four hours of sleep under her belt. Still, I enjoy my fleeting delusions.

Attitude plays a big part in how we feel about getting older. It can be a challenge to feel positive about living to a ripe old age in today's society. I love the famous retort made by Ronald Reagan during a debate when he was asked about his advanced age and quipped that he would not exploit Walter Mondale's "youth and inexperience."

But how can anyone deny the fact that a bright youthful countenance and toned body trumps a saggy wrinkled physique? I like to imagine that I could pass for a much younger person if you glimpsed me from behind. But reality would set in real fast as soon as I turned around and you glanced at my face. There's no hiding my advanced years there. Since I don't want the puffer fish look and would like to be able to fully close my eyes, I'm not hiding my imperfections with remedies like botox or plastic surgery. I just apply a modest amount of makeup so I don't scare people.

Many studies demonstrate that once you start feeling old, you start acting the part. Some people just start doing a lot less and living in a boring routine that typically consists of mega-doses of television, overeating and drinking, and napping on the couch. They convince themselves that they can no longer do certain things, so they don't bother to try anything new. When they get together with friends the conversation devolves into a whine-fest about painful body parts and recent surgeries.

I'm not joining that herd. Instead, I will continue to refuse to give into the Old Lady! I am defiant about this. I will never be a Leisure World-er. Nor will I grace the entrances of stores like Chico's, which, to me, reek of old lady.

Instead, I am going to keep my good habits of eating healthy food and putting in challenging daily workouts even though some of my body parts are definitely looking a little droopy and my old muscles look a bit scrawny compared to their younger version. Despite my brother telling me that I could benefit from eating a few cheeseburgers, I refuse to subscribe to the theory that it's OK to pack on extra pounds in case of a health emergency. I prefer to maintain my aura of a lean mean fighting machine.

## What Retirement Means to Me

I don't get the concept of retirement. It's just not part of my world view. The idea of retiring strikes fear in my heart because I associate it with sitting down and waiting for the arrival of the grim reaper. I've never met a hobby that I liked, don't have any grand kids to babysit, and would get violently ill and claustrophobic on a cruise.

What would I do if I gave up my business and my career? What purpose would I be fulfilling in life? Maybe it's my over-achieving Jewish upbringing, but I only feel satisfied if I know I have done something useful with each and every day.

Luckily I have a job that requires only a working brain and a big mouth. As long as my cognitive abilities remain intact and I can still put two semi-intelligent sentences together, Lorie Eber Wellness Coaching will be open for business and taking on new clients.

## Dealing with Normal Aging and Ailments

I often wonder if it's an asset or a detriment to have learned about Gerontology, the study of the aging process, since I know a lot about how the body ages and it isn't pretty. The body is designed to be at its peak when we are in our 20s and early 30s, our prime procreation years. Then it begins a long, slow degradation process. How is that for a succinct reality gut punch?

I didn't have to face this disheartening reality until recently. But at age 68, middle-age is in my rear view mirror. There are quite a few depressing expressions for this phase of life, like "over the hill," a Hallmark card favorite back in the day when we bought birthday cards.

There is no denying that I'm no longer blessed with the limber, strong body

I used to have. Now it screams for rest, recovery, and lots of TLC just to keep functioning without pain or injury. I can no longer stride into the gym, hoist some man-sized free weights for awhile, and go home with a buff physique. Now I live in fear of pulling a muscle or developing a repetitive stress injury that will torment me for the next year. In the good old days it would have healed in one week flat. I've been forced to make sissy stretch bands my new best friends so I can safely build muscle with considerably less risk of hurting myself. On the upside, I now feel fully justified in indulging in 90-minute deep tissue massages and paying for assisted stretching.

I have arthritis in my hands so I have no grip strength. But I've learned that there are a multitude of tools for that, including "Honey can you open this for me?" Occasionally, against my better judgment, and only if my husband isn't paying attention, I resort to my teeth.

Speaking of teeth, mine are showing their age. It seems like every week something is falling out. It might be just an old filling that needs replacement, but equally likely is that it's part of a tooth that finally gave up the ghost. In a desperate effort to minimize my drill time in the chair, I've tried a Waterpik and an electric toothbrush and hated them both. Sometimes I wonder why dentists don't work on retainer agreements or at least schedule standing weekly appointments.

One blessing I enjoy is that through some miracle of genetics or circumstance, I still don't have enough gray hair to waste three hours at the hair dresser every month camouflaging the color.

So far the only medication I take is an iron pill which I probably wouldn't need if I'd eat red meat which I've shunned since childhood because it requires too much chewing and I don't like seeing blood on my dinner plate.

## What Does the Future Hold?

While no one can accurately predict how they will age, I'm going to do my part to go "healthy, healthy, healthy, dead." If you have a better idea, please send it my way.

**2024**
RESOLUTION:

# | 14 |

## Holiday Musings

G rowing up in New York City yielded some unique holiday experiences. Trick-or-treating meant walking from floor to floor in our high-rise apartment building and not having to contend with the elements. Talk about convenient!

Another memory is the frustration of trying to fulfill the mandate of my Catholic high school to sell Christmas cards to the all Jewish people that lived in our building. It was a no-go. Year after year, after I completed my rounds of rejection, my Dad always ended up making a monetary contribution that he could ill afford.

Ironically, when I was in my 50s and my Dad was cognitively impaired, I learned that he was the son of very religious Russian Jewish parents. Imagine my surprise after having been told that we were German Catholics our whole lives. But that's a story for another day.

### Reflections

I do not consider myself a sentimentalist but I believe that the rituals we practice on holidays like Thanksgiving and Christmas hold a special place in our hearts. Whether good or bad, these experiences are part of our personal histories and they stick in our brains like peanut butter adheres to the roof of your mouth. One lesson I've learned over the years is that these observances are bound to evolve over time and my best bet is to gracefully adapt to the changes. So, without further ado, please allow me to share some of my holiday reflections.

## Gobble Gobble Except for Vegetarians

I remember childhood Thanksgivings as less than joyous occasions. My family definitely did not sit around the table sharing thoughts of appreciation and gratitude with one another. My mother was a reluctant cook at best and did not embrace the chore of whipping up a big holiday dinner with five kids underfoot. So she took as many shortcuts as possible. We feasted on canned vegetables, dried out turkey, and defrosted pumpkin pie. Neither parent made an effort to share their family traditions or special recipes and not a single relative or friend ever joined us. As far as I was concerned, a good Thanksgiving was one we got through with the bickering kept to a low simmer.

At some point, my mother put her foot down and refused to be responsible for making the special meal. If I needed a reminder that we were not a Norman Rockwell family, that did it. So we began eating out on Thanksgiving. While the tastiness metric increased, it felt like a lame cop-out.

Once I was a single adult, I usually went to my older brother's house, which was nearby, and had a pleasant experience catching up and enjoying a traditional feast cooked by his wife, who is an excellent chef.

After I got married and bought a house in San Rafael, I designated myself Turkey Day host. I'm not sure I fully appreciated the gravity of the undertaking when I raised my hand. At the time, I was a vegetarian who did not eat meat, fish, or fowl. However, I'd kept dairy products in my eating repertoire so as not to exclude my favorite sweet treats. I had belatedly learned to cook by watching TV shows and I was a purist. I insisted on making everything from scratch, including soaking beans overnight and engaging in a county-wide search for fresh produce and exotic herbs and spices every weekend.

I went all out to impress my mother-in-law and my brother's family every Thanksgiving. I even took a day off from slaving away as a lawyer to create the best experience for my guests. This was a one woman show. My husband was boogie boarding in the ocean while I spent two days in the kitchen laboriously whipping up what I hoped would be a delectable array of special holiday dishes.

I roasted a fresh Diestel turkey and made gravy for the "normal eaters," and also created a dazzling array of tasty vegetarian side dishes. I insisted on making the cranberry sauce and pumpkin pies from scratch. I instructed my guests not to bring anything other than flowers or wine. This was not a pot luck. I felt quite accomplished when the festive table was artfully arranged with my culinary achievements.

When the celebration was over and all the dishes were back in the cupboards, I felt the way Taylor Swift must feel after putting on one of her trademark super-high-energy four hour concerts. Thinking back on it now, I suspect my over-the-top efforts may have been a subconscious attempt to make up for what was lacking in my childhood.

Times and circumstance change. These days Wes and I go to his golf club and choose judiciously from the bountiful buffet while enjoying the beautifully decorated holiday-themed environment. It's a nice excuse to dress up and enjoy the special day without having to lift a finger or be burdened with tempting leftovers.

## Christmas or Festivus

As a child, Christmas was naturally the premier holiday in our household. Nowadays it seems to have become mandatory, at least in California, to acknowledge not only the Christian version but every other comparable holiday celebration by name, lest we offend someone. I have rebelled and taken to jokingly offering the alternative of Festivus in a nod to *Seinfeld*.

I have some fond memories of Christmas. The first one that comes to mind is the clever ploy my Dad invented to lighten the task of holiday shopping. In retrospect, it occurs to me that his background as a college Economics Instructor may have spawned this brilliant notion.

As I told you in Chapter 1, my Dad solved some holiday headaches by using the giant Sears catalog which was filled with page after page of children's toys complete with mail order prices. He gave each of us a budget and let us make our own selections. This avoided Christmas morning disappointment syndrome, unless the chosen item was out of stock. Still, his clever idea was the perfect problem solver for kid satisfaction and cost control.

My other lasting memory is of Christmas Day. My Dad told us that Santa liked milk and cookies, so we made sure his reward for descending the chimney was conspicuously placed on the kitchen counter as a thank you. When we got up at the crack of dawn, the milk glass was empty and only a few crumbs remained; proof that Santa had left gifts under the tree. I also remember one year when I convinced myself that Saint Nick had moved my slippers. It was fun to be young and naïve.

Once I realized that Santa was a fantasy, the holiday lost some of its luster. It was still fun but as a workaholic lawyer, I found it stressful to find the time to visit overcrowded brick and mortar retailers looking for the perfect gifts for family, close friends, and colleagues. The best I could hope for was that I had purchased at least a few non-regifters.

There were also a number of December 25ths I'd just as soon lose from my memory banks. One year my older brother decided the family needed to spend the holiday together in Lake Tahoe. He rented a house near the slopes and hoped we'd all have a good time skiing and lounging in front of a roaring fire. Despite his good intentions it went bad. My Dad pouted the whole time and stayed alone at the house each day because he'd never learned to ski. He refused to even go to the slopes and drink hot chocolate. To make matters worse, my Mother ended up in the ER on Christmas Eve with a fractured wrist that she claimed never healed properly.

Another year, I was the one who pouted and ended up bored and lonely. At the time I was married to my first husband who was raised in a very religious close-knit Italian family. The clan attended early Midnight Mass before enjoying a big Christmas dinner. I was non-religious and didn't want to feel like a fraud sitting through mass, so I chose to have a miserable time sitting in the cold empty house by myself waiting for them to return after they'd been duly blessed.

Some of my happier memories are of visits to Manhattan perusing its dazzling department store windows and taking pictures with the majestic Rockefeller Plaza tree as a backdrop. Then we'd drive upstate to join my sister and watch my niece and nephew excitedly tear into a truly excessive number of gifts under a picture perfect Christmas tree.

Now that I have become a reluctant traveler and have less tolerance for cold weather, my husband and I have started a new tradition. We drive to our favorite resort lodge situated within an hour of our home and enjoy the festive atmosphere replete with visiting carolers and infused with the scent of a wood burning fireplace.

# | 15 |

## New Year's Resolutions

Do you make New Year's resolutions? As many as 40 percent of Americans do and many report feeling pressured to do so. Predictably, every year the most common areas of hoped for change relate to ditching weight and moving more.

Next question: Do you actually achieve the goals that you've set for the new year? If so, you are the rare exception. The statistics heavily predict failure. In fact, 80 percent of these well-intentioned pledges are abandoned by the end of February.

There are many reasons why these aspirations do not pan out. Some pledges are vague and non-specific, while others are too rigid and unrealistically aggressive. But the biggest obstacle is staying focused on health while juggling all the balls we call daily life. Often one curve ball can relegate the resolution into the litter pile. Then you can try again next year.

### I Never Make New Year's Resolutions

Perhaps one of the reasons I'm so jaded with regard to yearly goals comes from my 24 years of experience as a gym rat. Every January the gym would be invaded by new members who'd signed up for personal training sessions. As a committed regular, I viewed this sudden influx as an annoying interference with my workout routine. The equipment that was normally readily available was now being monopolized by newbies who were violating my hard earned squatters rights.

But a few years of experience taught me that this phenomenon fit the Ivory Soap purity equation. By mid-February, when their 6-week personal training package expired, 99.44 percent of these intruders were gone. My educated guess is that the vast majority of these gym rookies left disappointed by the fact that they did not lose any weight despite the intense training sessions which they assumed would incinerate that loathsome body fat. They probably blamed their trainers, not knowing that the jaw muscle is the one that controls the weight loss.

I certainly don't want to denigrate anyone who takes the time to think about the year ahead and aspires to live a better life in some way that would make them a happier human. I think that's wonderful.

But for me resolutions feel like an exercise in futility. I'm more of an impatient "Just Do It!" person. No need to talk about it, just start, fail most of the time, and get back up. I just keep showing up with my mega dose of determination and I seem to get where I want to go.

## Predicting the Future is a Zero Sum Game

I'm not only a naysayer when it comes to New Year's resolutions. I have applied my reticence to set goal posts to both my legal career and my wellness business. My justification is based on my belief that there are too many things out of my control that can affect whatever outcome I am trying to achieve. My crystal ball has been in the shop for some time and seems to be a lemon. I'm more likely to blow a few bucks on a lottery ticket for the $2 billion jackpot than to prognosticate about the course of my future.

I'd rather focus my energies on tackling each hurdle head-on and adroitly pivoting around any roadblocks I encounter.

## No Career Planning in My Legal Career

The closest I've ever come to goal setting was my pigheadedness about becoming a partner in my law firm. And that was really less about planning and more about proving to myself that I could achieve the status I felt I deserved.

To the extent that I had a plan, it turned out to be wrong-headed. I went with the typical naïve girl assumption that getting into the club was something to be earned with hard work. I was not privy to the primer that taught about acquiring a mentor and bragging up my accomplishments. I had no idea how to cajole a group of alpha male attorneys into opening the door to their private port-drinking, cigar-puffing get togethers.

My law firm represented the defense side of cases and got paid based on the number of hours the attorneys billed to each matter. I leapt to the erroneous conclusion that being the highest biller in the firm year after year was my key to the pearly gates. So I worked my butt off to the point of sacrificing a personal life. The result: I was passed over for partnership for 4 years with no explanation.

In Chapter 2, I told you the story of how I finally greased the skids and was awarded entry into the club. If I had known that my personal version of *Extreme Makeover* was the ticket to success, it might have happened a lot sooner.

How's that for career planning? I wouldn't have imagined that this superficial change was all that had been holding me back from my dream of making partner regardless of how much time I might have devoted to setting yearly New Year's resolutions. Nor could I have predicted that I'd open the firm's only branch office and that eight years later I'd decide to relegate the practice of law to the rear view mirror.

## I'm Still the Anti-Planner

After I escaped legal practice, I made a decision that I was going to enjoy an easier life in my second career. No more beating my head against the wall in the quest to prove to myself that I was worthy. That was behind me.

I adopted the approach that if a door that I tried did not yield to slight pressure, I would move on and keep looking for one that was open. That mental make-over led to a 10-year long self-evolution that turned out to be a very freeing and fulfilling journey. I'm pleased to report that the end result was a kinder, gentler version of myself than the one I formerly presented as a hard-driven lawyer. I was amazed and relieved to discover that I had many other skills and talents ripe for development.

I didn't plan anything. Instead I sequentially explored gerontology, elder care, public speaking, creative writing, and finally landed on wellness coaching. When I started my journey I had no idea that my chosen field even existed.

## No Yearly Business Plan for Me

When I started my wellness coaching business everyone told me that the first thing a responsible businessperson does is draft a business plan. The main goal of the exercise seemed to be to set monetary targets for the year. I have to admit that I never even put finger to keyboard to draft such a blueprint. I knew that I didn't have the foresight to even guesstimate how many clients might sign up or how much money my business would generate in a year.

I certainly did not see the Covid business-killer shut-downs coming in 2020. Nor did I anticipate the severe economic downturn in 2022. Both had a severe impact on small businesses like mine. But do you suppose either event was accounted for in anyone's business plan for those years?

Despite my lack of planning, I stumbled onto my mission of helping people get healthier and improve their lives.

## Bucket List Anyone?

My life has certainly been filled with unplanned events like meeting my husband and experiencing "love at first sight," a phenomenon I was certain did not exist. I don't know what's waiting for me around the next corner. But I do know this—I'm not ready to start compiling my bucket list.

# Conclusion

We all have interesting and unexpected experiences. How we handle each curve ball, hurdle, and surprise determines the quality of our lives. As you now know, I am a striver who has never shied away from dealing with the problems that have arisen in my life.

Undoubtedly the biggest obstacle that I powered through was making partner in a male dominated law firm. I was distraught when I kept getting passed over for entry into the inner sanctum and befuddled as to how to unlock that door. Many women would have bailed and gotten an of-counsel position with another firm, but I was fixated on reaching a goal that I'd set for myself decades earlier. I finally got what I wanted through dogged perseverance and I now understand that what propelled me was a need to prove to myself that I was capable of achieving a status that conferred societal respect.

Dealing with chronic pain turned out to be an unexpected challenge that felt unfairly inflicted on me, especially since I work hard at taking good care of my body. I've soldiered through several extended bouts of agony and learned how all-consuming it can be. When just trying to do normal activities brings you to tears, you go into survival mode, try not to cry all the time, and become extremely self-centered. My coping mechanism has been to busy my brain with other things so it has less time to focus on how much everything hurts. I imagine I will have to endure new and different injuries and ailments in the future, so I figure I've gotten a good head start.

The other challenge in my life, which I suspect is endemic in our society today is that we are running through life at warp speed, while trying to keep all the balls we're juggling up in the air. Our hurry up society seems to demand that we do more in less time. The sad result is that we are a stressed-out nation and have no time to attend to our health or to truly relax. We all need to smell more roses. After all, it's these small quiet interludes that bring us peace and joy.

# About the Author

Lorie Eber has had two very different careers. Career #1 was as a corporate litigator with a law firm in San Francisco. She persevered until she cleared all the hurdles and was allowed to enter the partnership ranks. A few years later, she volunteered to open a branch office in SoCal, which she managed and made quite successful.

But then came the curve ball. She fell in love with her perfect match and wasted no time tying the knot. After all, neither of them was getting any younger. Her fledgling marriage and diminishing enthusiasm for working non-stop in her stressful position made her rethink her priorities. She decided to bite the bullet and get brave, and announced her retirement from the firm at age 49. She had no clue what her next life endeavor might be and spent nearly 10 years searching until she landed on a vocation she was passionate about.

The path of self-discovery to identify career #2 was full of wonderful surprises, as Lorie discovered long hidden and undeveloped skills and talents she never knew were hiding under her tough-guy lawyer facade.

Career #2 is Wellness Coaching. It's a perfect fit because Lorie believes that poor health and unhealthy lifestyles are the real pandemic. This is evidenced by the fact that 75 percent of all Americans are now overweight or obese.

Her business, Lorie Eber Wellness Coaching, is now 11 years old. She provides customized and personalized weight loss and healthy living coaching and support both in her office or online. Ms. Eber's approach is to partner with her clients as they work on improving their health habits. She uses her unique style of straight-talk, cracking the whip, and dispensing empathy as appropriate. She often reminds her clients that achieving a healthy lifestyle is the ultimate struggle in today's world, which is driven by convenience and immediate gratification. Unfortunately, we often use food for emotional gratification rather than as fuel for our bodies. Much of our relaxation and socializing center around eating huge portions of restaurant prepared food flavored with copious amounts of butter and oil. In this environment, accountability and advice from an expert have become almost indispensable for achieving long-lasting behavior change.

Lorie is well trained in her new field. She is a Certified Nutritionist and NASM Personal Trainer. She holds a certification in Nutrition Science from the Stanford University Center for Health Education, and is a Mayo Clinic Certified Wellness Coach. She is also credentialed by Wellcoaches School of Coaching and is a trained life coach. She recently earned her nationwide certification as a National Board-Certified Health & Wellness Coach.

Being the overachiever that she is, Lorie also has a second job as an Instructor of Health and Aging Studies at Coastline College. Fortunately, the new Dean is interested in the health and wellness field and has allowed Lorie to create two wellness coaching courses which she now teaches online.

Lorie doesn't just talk-the-talk; she also walks-the-walk. She works hard to model the behaviors she preaches. She works out strenuously every day except Sunday, which she takes as a rest day. Her workouts include strength training, running on a dirt trail in the park, taking treadmill classes at a gym, and riding her Peloton bike. Her diet emphasizes God-made foods and minimizes man-made foods. It is largely plant-based, centered around fruits and vegetables. It highlights lean proteins like fish and chicken and whole grains for energy.

While exercising and eating well are second nature, stress reduction continues to be a work in progress for Lorie. But she has successfully incorporated Chill Out Sundays into her weekly routine to rejuvenate. On those days, she takes long walks and gets pampered with either a massage or an assisted stretch from her trainer. Then she sits outside in the sunshine with her Cold Brew and reads non-fiction to relax.

Lorie Eber has previously published nine books available on Amazon as paperbacks and e-Books:

*How to Get Out of Your Food Coma and Get Healthy*

*How I Escaped Legal Practice and Got Myself a Life*

*Why I'm Not a Fat Old Lady*

*How to Ditch Your Fat Clothes for Good*

*40 Ways to Leave Your Lover: That Would be Junk Food*

*How to Stay Healthy in a World Designed to Make Us Fat and Lazy*

*Aging Beats the Alternative and a Sense of Humor Helps*

*How to Tell Food Who's Boss: A Step-By-Step Guide*

*Ready to Forsake Your Couch Potato Junk Food Eating Ways?*

For more information about Lorie and the lifestyle-enhancing services she offers, visit her website:

# www.LorieEberWellnessCoaching.com

Made in the USA
Columbia, SC
07 August 2024

39707551R00063